NIST Special Publication 800-100

Information Security Handbook: A Guide for Managers

NIST
National Institute of Standards and Technology
Technology Administration
U.S. Department of Commerce

Recommendations of the National Institute of Standards and Technology

Pauline Bowen
Joan Hash
Mark Wilson

INFORMATION SECURITY

Computer Security Division
Information Technology Laboratory
National Institute of Standards and Technology
Gaithersburg, MD 20899-8930

October 2006

U.S. Department of Commerce
Carlos M. Gutierrez, Secretary

Technology Administration
Robert Cresanti, Under Secretary of Commerce for Technology

National Institute of Standards and Technology
William Jeffrey, Director

Reports on Information Systems Technology

The Information Technology Laboratory (ITL) at the National Institute of Standards and Technology promotes the U.S. economy and public welfare by providing technical leadership for the Nation's measurement and standards infrastructure. ITL develops tests, test methods, reference data, proof-of-concept implementations, and technical analyses to advance the development and productive use of information technology. ITL's responsibilities include the development of management, administrative, technical, and physical standards and guidelines for the cost-effective security and privacy of nonnational-security-related information in federal information systems. This Special Publication 800 series reports on ITL's research, guidelines, and outreach efforts in information system security and its collaborative activities with industry, government, and academic organizations.

Authority

This document has been developed by the National Institute of Standards and Technology (NIST) in furtherance of its statutory responsibilities under the Federal Information Security Management Act (FISMA) of 2002, Public Law 107-347.

NIST is responsible for developing standards and guidelines, including minimum requirements, and for providing adequate information security for all agency operations and assets, but such standards and guidelines shall not apply to national security systems. This guideline is consistent with the requirements of the Office of Management and Budget (OMB) Circular A-130, Section 8b(3), *Securing Agency Information Systems*, as analyzed in A-130, Appendix IV: *Analysis of Key Sections*. Supplemental information is provided A-130, Appendix III.

This guideline has been prepared for use by federal agencies. It may also be used by nongovernmental organizations on a voluntary basis and is not subject to copyright regulations. (Attribution would be appreciated by NIST.)

Nothing in this document should be taken to contradict standards and guidelines made mandatory and binding on federal agencies by the Secretary of Commerce under statutory authority. Nor should these guidelines be interpreted as altering or superseding the existing authorities of the Secretary of Commerce, Director of the OMB, or any other federal official.

Certain commercial entities, equipment, or materials may be identified in this document in order to describe an experimental procedure or concept adequately. Such identification is not intended to imply recommendation or endorsement by NIST, nor is it intended to imply that the entities, materials, or equipment are necessarily the best available for the purpose.

Acknowledgements

NIST would like to thank the many people who assisted with the development of this handbook.

NIST management officials who supported this effort include: Joan Hash, William C. Barker, Elizabeth Chew, and Matthew Scholl.

The authors would like to thank Elizabeth Lennon, Alicia Clay, Elizabeth Chew, Richard Kissel, Carol Schmidt, Matthew Scholl, and Patricia Toth who assisted with reviewing this Handbook and provided comments and suggestions for improvement.

Additional drafters of Handbook chapters include:

Ron Ross, Tim Grance, and Marianne Swanson, NIST.

Nadya Bartol, Joe Nusbaum, Laura Prause, Will Robinson, Karen Kent, and Randy Ewell, BAH,

In addition, special thanks are due those contractors who helped craft the Handbook, prepare drafts, and review materials:

Nadya Bartol of Booz, Allen, Hamiliton (BAH), served as Project Manager for BAH on this project. In addition, many BAH employees contributed to the Handbook, including: Anthony Brown, Linda Duncan, Gina Jamaldinian, Sedar Labarre, Ines Murphy, Steven Peck, Mike Kapetanovic, Michael Rohde, Jacob Tsizis, Aderonke Adeniji, and Marge Spanninger.

The authors also gratefully acknowledge and appreciate the many contributions from individuals in the public and private sectors whose thoughtful and constructive comments improved the quality and usefulness of this publication.

Errata

The following changes have been incorporated into Special Publication 800-100.

1. Chapter 10 Risk Management, Figure 10-1. Risk Management in the System Security Life Cycle diagram has been modified to remove numbers from diagram and to show the steps clearly in the risk management process in the system security life cycle.

2. Chapter 10 Risk Management, Table 10-1. Risk Level Matrix has been modified to correct the math in the diagram.

Table of Contents

Chapter 1

1. Introduction

This Information Security Handbook provides a broad overview of information security program elements to assist managers in understanding how to establish and implement an information security program. Typically, the organization looks to the program for overall responsibility to ensure the selection and implementation of appropriate security controls and to demonstrate the effectiveness of satisfying their stated security requirements. The topics within this document were selected based on the laws and regulations relevant to information security, including the Clinger-Cohen Act of 1996, the Federal Information Security Management Act (FISMA) of 2002, and Office of Management and Budget (OMB) Circular A-130. The material in this handbook can be referenced for general information on a particular topic or can be used in the decision-making process for developing an information security program. National Institute of Standards and Technology (NISTIR) Interagency Report 7298 provides a summary glossary for the basic security terms used throughout this document. While reading this handbook, please consider that the guidance is not specific to a particular agency. Agencies should tailor this guidance according to their security posture and business requirements.

1.1   Purpose and Applicability

The purpose of this publication is to inform members of the information security management team (agency heads; chief information officers [CIOs]; senior agency information security officers [SAISOs], also commonly referred to as Chief Information Security Officers [CISOs]; and security managers) about various aspects of information security that they will be expected to implement and oversee in their respective organizations. In addition, the handbook provides guidance for facilitating a more consistent approach to information security programs across the federal government. Even though the terminology in this document is geared toward the federal sector, the handbook can also be used to provide guidance on a variety of other governmental, organizational, or institutional security requirements.

1.2   Relationship to Existing Guidance

This handbook summarizes and augments a number of existing NIST standards and guidance documents and provides additional information on related topics. Such documents are referenced within appropriate subchapters.

1.3   Audience

The intended audience includes agency heads, CIOs, SAISOs (also commonly referred to as CISOs), and security managers. The handbook provides information that the audience can use in building their information security program strategy. While there are differences between federal and private sector environments, especially in terms of priorities and legal requirements, the underlying principles of information security are the same. The handbook is therefore useful to any manager who requires a broad overview of information security practices.

Chapter 2

2. Information Security Governance

Federal agencies rely heavily on information technology (IT) to run their daily operations and deliver products and services. With an increasing reliability on IT, a growing complexity of federal government IT infrastructure, and a constantly changing information security threat and risk environment, information security has become a mission-essential function. This function must be managed and governed to reduce the risks to federal government operations and to ensure the federal government's ability to do business and serve the American public.

The purpose of information security governance is to ensure that agencies are proactively implementing appropriate information security controls to support their mission in a cost-effective manner, while managing evolving information security risks. As such, information security governance has its own set of requirements, challenges, activities, and types of possible structures. Information security governance also has a defining role in identifying key information security roles and responsibilities, and it influences information security policy development and oversight and ongoing monitoring activities.

To ensure an appropriate level of support of agency missions and the proper implementation of current and future information security requirements, each agency should establish a formal information security governance structure.

Information security governance can be defined as the process of establishing and maintaining a framework and supporting management structure and processes to provide assurance that information security strategies are aligned with and support business objectives, are consistent with applicable laws and regulations through adherence to policies and internal controls, and provide assignment of responsibility, all in an effort to manage risk.

2.1 Information Security Governance Requirements

The United States (U.S.) Congress and the Office of Management and Budget (OMB) have instituted a number of laws, regulations, and directives that govern establishment and implementation of federal information security practices. These laws, regulations, and directives establish federal- and agency-level responsibilities for information security, define key information security roles and responsibilities, identify minimum information security controls, specify compliance reporting rules and procedures, and provide other essential requirements and guidance. These laws and regulations place responsibility and accountability for information security at all levels within federal agencies, from the agency head to IT users. They also provide an infrastructure for developing and promulgating detailed standards and implementation guidance to federal agencies and overseeing implementation of required practices through NIST and the Government Accountability Office (GAO), respectively.

These three entities, the U.S. Congress, OMB, and GAO, define and influence federal agency governance and information security requirements. Congress creates laws and oversight measures to establish objectives, present timely analyses to establish overall governance standards across the federal government, and provide aid in economic and budget decisions, including decisions about public IT assets and those funds needed to secure them. Agencies must establish clear reporting requirements that meet legislative requirements set by Congress and must also provide Congress with the necessary information and estimates required for the congressional budget process. OMB assists the President in overseeing the preparation of the federal budget and supervises its administration by the executive branch agencies. OMB provides further guidance to the agencies on implementing legislative information requirements in the form of circulars and memoranda. GAO also provides oversight of agency information security activities as a part of its mission "to support the Congress in meeting its constitutional responsibilities and to help improve the performance and ensure the accountability of the federal government for the benefit of the American people."[1] GAO reviews agency implementation of legislative and regulatory requirements and reports to Congress and the American public on its findings.

At a minimum, information security governance in a federal department or agency must meet the requirements as they are detailed in applicable legislation, regulations, and directives. Furthermore, agencies can benefit from identifying overall good governance practices for establishing strong management and oversight. Agencies should tailor their information security governance practices to their organization's own missions, operations, and needs.

The following are a few key legislative acts that define overall federal agency governance requirements:

- The Government Performance and Results Act (GPRA) of 1993 establishes the foundation for budget decision making to achieve strategic goals in order to meet agency mission objectives.

- The Paperwork Reduction Act (PRA) of 1995 requires agencies to perform their information resource management activities in an efficient, effective, and economical manner.

- The Federal Financial Management Improvement Act (FFMIA) of 1996 requires accountability of financial and program managers for financial results of actions taken, control over the federal government's financial resources, and protection of federal assets.

- The Federal Managers Financial Integrity Act (FMFIA) of 1982 requires ongoing evaluations and reports from each executive on the adequacy of administrative control for internal accounting systems.

- The Clinger-Cohen Act of 1996 requires agencies to use a disciplined capital planning and investment control (CPIC) process to acquire, use, maintain, and dispose of IT resources, and establishes a role of chief information officer (CIO) within each federal agency.

- The E-Government Act of 2002 (Public Law 107-347) promotes better use of the Internet and other IT resources to improve government services for citizens and internal government operations, and provide opportunities for citizen participation in government. The Act also requires agencies to:
  - Comply with FISMA, included as Title III of the E-Government Act;
  - Support governmentwide e-government initiatives;
  - Leverage cross-agency opportunities to further e-government through the Federal Enterprise Architecture (FEA) initiative; and

---

[1] GAO, GAO-04-534SP, 'GAO Strategic Plan 2004-2009,' March 2004.

    – Conduct and submit to OMB privacy impact assessments for all new IT investments administering information in identifiable form collected from or about members of the public.

Supporting these acts, three legislative documents emerge as the foundational sources for specific information security governance requirements:

- The Federal Information Security Management (FISMA) Act is the primary legislation governing federal information security programs, building upon earlier legislation through added emphasis on the management dimension of information security.

  – FISMA delegates to the National Institute of Standards and Technology (NIST) the responsibility to develop detailed information security standards and guidance for federal information systems, with the exception of national security systems.

  – FISMA designates to OMB the oversight of federal agencies' information security implementation.

  – FISMA provides a comprehensive framework for securing federal government IT resources, including defining key federal government and agency roles and responsibilities, requiring agencies to integrate information security into their capital planning and enterprise architecture processes, requiring agencies to conduct annual information security reviews of all programs and systems, and reporting the results of those reviews to OMB.[2]

- OMB Circular A-130, *Management of Federal Information Resources*, Appendix III, *Security of Federal Automated Information Resources*, establishes a minimum set of controls to be included in federal automated information security programs, assigns federal agency responsibilities for the security of automated information, and links agency automated information security programs and agency management control systems.[3]

- Homeland Security Presidential Directive 12 (HSPD-12), released in August 2004, specifies a "policy for a common identification standard for all Federal employees and contractors."[4] HSPD-12 intends to increase identification security and interoperability by standardizing the process to issue a Federal employee or contractor an identification credential, and also by specifying the electronic and physical properties of the credential itself. The HSPD-12 credential is known as the Personal Identity Verification card.

Figure 2-1 illustrates key roles of legislative, regulatory, and oversight bodies in establishing governance and information security governance requirements for the federal enterprise.

---

[2] FISMA, H.R. 2458–48, 'Federal Information Security Management Act,' 2002.
[3] OMB, 'Office of Management and Budget Circular A-130, Appendix III,' 1996.
[4] OMB, M-05-24, 'Implementation of Homeland Security Presidential Directive (HSPD) 12 – Policy for a Common Identification Standard for Federal Employees and Contractors.'

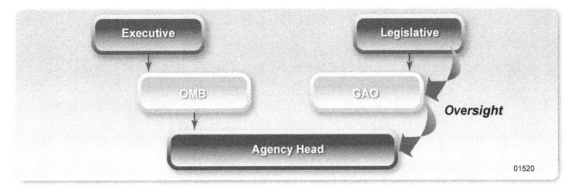

Figure 2-1. Key Legislative, Regulatory, and Oversight Roles

The need to identify and implement appropriate federal government and agency-specific information security governance practices can be daunting. Agencies should identify applicable requirements based on relevant legislation, regulations, federal directives, and agency-level directives. Agencies should also ensure that information security governance structures are implemented in a manner that best supports their unique missions and operations.

2.2 Information Security Governance Components

Agencies should integrate their information security governance activities with the overall agency structure and activities by ensuring appropriate participation of agency officials in overseeing implementation of information security controls throughout the agency. The key activities that facilitate such integration are strategic planning, organizational design and development, establishment of roles and responsibilities, integration with the enterprise architecture, and documentation of security objectives in policies and guidance. Figure 2-2 illustrates the relative relationship of these various components.

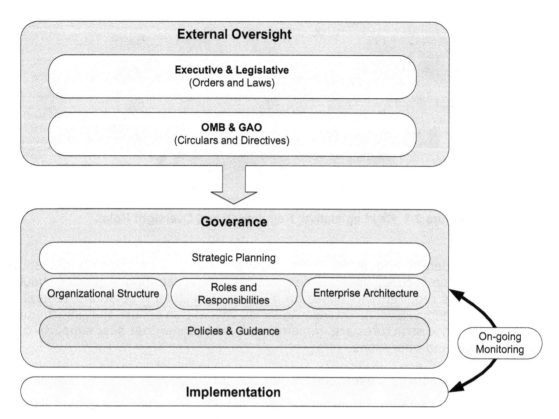

Figure 2-2. Information Security Governance Components

2.2.1 Information Security Strategic Planning

"Strategic plans, annual performance plans, and annual program performance reports are the main elements of GPRA. Together these elements create a recurring cycle of reporting, planning, and execution."[5]

GPRA requires federal agencies to develop and submit to OMB and Congress a "strategic plan for program activities" and "prepare an annual performance plan covering each program activity set forth in the budget of such agency."[6] Agencies are required to refresh their strategic plans within three years of submitting their previous strategic plans, while submitting performance plans is required annually.

Agencies should integrate information security into the agency strategic planning processes by establishing and documenting information security strategies that directly support agency strategic and performance planning activities. The organization's information security strategy should establish a comprehensive framework to enable the development, institutionalization, assessment, and improvement of the agency's information security program. The information security strategy should support the overall agency strategic and performance plans and IT strategic plan (if applicable) with its content clearly traceable to these higher-level sources. Each agency should define the following for its information security program:

---

[5] OMB, 'Office of Management and Budget Circular A-130 Appendix III,' 1996.
[6] OMB, Section 306, 'Government Performance and Results Act' (GPRA), 1993.

- Clear and comprehensive mission, vision, goals, and objectives and how they relate to agency mission;

- High-level plan for achieving information security goals and objectives, including short- and mid-term objectives and performance targets, specific for each goal and objective, to be used throughout the life of this plan to manage progress toward successfully fulfilling the identified objectives; and

- Performance measures to continuously monitor accomplishment of identified goals and objectives and their progress toward stated targets.

Agencies should document their information security strategy in an information security strategic plan or another document, if appropriate. Regardless of how the information security strategy is documented, its contents should be aligned with the overall agency strategic planning activities. The document should be revisited when a major change in the agency information security environment occurs, including:

- Change in applicable legislation, regulations, or directives;
- Change in agency mission priorities; and
- Emerging information security issues, such as changes in threat and vulnerability environment or the introduction of new technologies.

2.2.2 Information Security Governance Structures

Information security governance structures can be characterized in a number of ways. There are two basic models of information security governance structures: centralized and decentralized. While agency heads are ultimately responsible for managing and governing their respective agency, the authority and responsibility over information security differs in the two types of structures. Key characteristics of the two structures are:

- **Centralized.** Departmental CIO or, in some instances, the SAISO has line-item budget control over all information security activities throughout the department. All information security practitioners within the department report to the departmental SAISO, who is responsible for ensuring implementation and monitoring of information security controls throughout the entire department.

- **Decentralized.** Departmental SAISOs have policy development and oversight responsibilities. Departmental SAISOs have budget responsibilities over the departmental information security program, but not over the operating units' information security programs. Operating unit SAISOs report to the unit head, not to the departmental SAISO. Operating unit SAISOs are responsible for implementing and monitoring information security practices within their respective operating units.

Completely centralized or decentralized information security governance implementations are quite rare. In reality, the variety of implemented information security governance structures spans the continuum from a centralized structure at one end to a decentralized structure at the other. Agencies usually adopt hybrid structures that include some characteristics of both centralized and decentralized types of structures, and they adopt the particular mix of these characteristics to fit their agency mission, size, homogeneity of their components, and existing governance structure.

Agencies in the process of establishing or changing their information security governance structure should consider the following key factors to determine the optimal extent of the centralization or decentralization:

- Agency size;
- Agency mission and its level of diversification or homogeneity;
- Existing agency IT infrastructure;
- Existing federal and internal governance requirements;
- Size of agency budget;
- Agency information security capabilities;
- Number of, and distance between, physical locations; and
- Decision-making practices and desired rate of change in information security practices.

To the degree that these factors are limited or varied, an organization's hybrid information security governance structure will fall somewhere between the extremes of a completely centralized or decentralized structure, as depicted in Figure 2-3. An organization's placement on this continuum may also shift over time in response to changing internal factors or external requirements.

Since information security governance structure is highly dependent on the overall organizational structure, organizations are often limited in their choices about how to organize their information security governance activities. Agencies should be cognizant of the characteristics and challenges that a centralized or decentralized structure presents and work within their respective organizations to ensure the best use of information security resources within the boundaries of their own structure.

2.2.3 Key Governance Roles and Responsibilities[7]

There are several governance stakeholders common to most organizations that span the organization. These stakeholders include senior leadership, a CIO, information security personnel, and a chief financial officer (CFO), among others. The specific requirements of each role may differ with the degree of information security governance centralization or in response to the specific missions and needs of an organization.

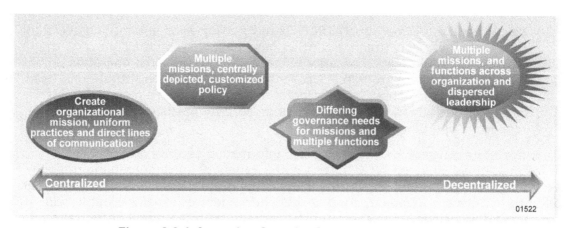

Figure 2-3. Information Security Governance Structures

---

[7] See Chapter 5, Capital Planning; Chapter 8, Security Planning; Chapter 11, Certification, Accreditation, and Security Assessments; and Chapter 14, Configuration Management; of this guide for additional guidance on system-specific security roles and responsibilities.

2.2.3.1 Agency Head

The Clinger-Cohen Act assigns the responsibility for ensuring "that the information security policies, procedures, and practices of the executive agency are adequate."[8] FISMA provides the following details on agency head responsibilities for information security:

- Providing information security protections commensurate with the risk and magnitude of the harm resulting from unauthorized access, use, disclosure, disruption, modification, or destruction of information collected or maintained by or on behalf of an agency, and on information systems used or operated by an agency or by a contractor of an agency or other organization on behalf of an agency;

- Ensuring that an information security program is developed, documented, and implemented to provide security for all systems, networks, and data that support the operations of the organization;

- Ensuring that information security processes are integrated with strategic and operational planning processes to secure the organization's mission;

- Ensuring that senior agency officials within the organization are given the necessary authority to secure the operations and assets under their control;

- Designating a CIO and delegating authority to that individual to ensure compliance with applicable information security requirements;

- Ensuring that the agency has trained personnel to support compliance with information security policies, processes, standards, and guidelines; and

- Ensuring that the CIO, in coordination with the other senior agency officials, reports annually to the agency head on the effectiveness of the agency information security program, including the progress of remedial actions.

2.2.3.2 Chief Information Officer

FISMA assigns the agency CIO the following responsibilities:

- Designating a senior agency information security officer (SAISO);

- Developing and maintaining an agency-wide information security program;

- Developing and maintaining information security policies, procedures, and control techniques to address all applicable requirements;

- Ensuring compliance with applicable information security requirements; and

- Reporting annually, in coordination with the other senior agency officials, to the agency head on the effectiveness of the agency information security program, including progress of remedial actions.

2.2.3.3 Senior Agency Information Security Officer[9]

FISMA assigns SAISO the following responsibilities:

- Performing information security duties as the primary duty;

---

[8] Clinger-Cohen Act, 1996.
[9] The SAISO in some agencies is sometimes referred to as the computer information security officer (CISO) or the chief security officer (CSO).

- Heading an office with the mission and resources to assist in ensuring agency compliance with information security requirements;

- Periodically assessing risk and magnitude of the harm resulting from unauthorized access, use, disclosure, disruption, modification, or destruction of information and information systems that support the operations and assets of the agency;

- Developing and maintaining risk-based, cost-effective information security policies, procedures, and control techniques to address all applicable requirements throughout the life cycle of each agency information system to ensure compliance with applicable requirements;

- Facilitating development of subordinate plans for providing adequate information security for networks, facilities, and systems or groups of information systems;

- Ensuring that agency personnel, including contractors, receive appropriate information security awareness training;

- Training and overseeing personnel with significant responsibilities for information security with respect to such responsibilities;

- Periodically testing and evaluating the effectiveness of information security policies, procedures, and practices;

- Establishing and maintaining a process for planning, implementing, evaluating, and documenting remedial action to address any deficiencies in the information security policies, procedures, and practices of the agency;

- Developing and implementing procedures for detecting, reporting, and responding to security incidents;

- Ensuring preparation and maintenance of plans and procedures to provide continuity of operations for information systems that support the operations and assets of the agency; and

- Supporting the agency CIO in annual reporting to the agency head on the effectiveness of the agency information security program, including progress of remedial actions.

2.2.3.4 Chief Enterprise Architect

The chief enterprise architect or comparable position in an organization is responsible for:

- Leading agency enterprise architecture development and implementation efforts;

- Collaborating with lines of business within the agency to ensure proper integration of lines of business into enterprise architecture;

- Participating in agency strategic planning and performance planning activities to ensure proper integration of enterprise architecture;

- Facilitating integration of information security into all layers of enterprise architecture to ensure agency implementation of secure solutions; and

- Working closely with the program managers, the senior agency information security officer (SAISO), and the business owners to ensure that all technical architecture requirements are adequately addressed by applying FEA and the Security and Privacy Profile (SPP).

2.2.3.5 Related Roles

Many other individuals within an organization have a stake in information security, from top senior management down to individual users. A few of the primary senior management roles and their coinciding responsibilities are listed below. The scope of each role will depend on whether or not these roles should be redundant in the decentralized governance structure. These individuals should work collaboratively to ensure that information security exists within their organizational responsibility.

Inspector General (IG). The IG is a statutory office within an organization that, in addition to other responsibilities, works to assess an organization's information security practices and identifies vulnerabilities and the possible need to modify security measures. The IG completes this task by:

- Detecting fraud or instances of waste, abuse, or misuse of an organization's funds;
- Identifying operational deficiencies within the organization;
- Ensuring that the underlying problems that permit such failings are rectified; and
- Offering recommendations for preventing problems in the future.

Chief Financial Officer. The CFO is the senior financial advisor to the investment review board (IRB) and the agency head. Information security investments fall within the purview of the CFO and are included in the CFO's reports. In this capacity, the CFO is responsible for:

- Reviewing cost goals of each major information security investment;
- Reporting financial management information to OMB as part of the President's budget;
- Complying with legislative and OMB-defined responsibilities as they relate to IT capital investments;
- Reviewing systems that impact financial management activities; and
- Forwarding investment assessments to the IRB.

Chief Privacy Officer or other designated official with privacy responsibilities. The chief privacy officer is responsible for privacy compliance across an organization, including privacy compliance measures that apply to information security assets and activities. The chief privacy officer works to maintain a balance between security and privacy requirements, and works to ensure that one is not compromised for the sake of the other. To this end, the chief privacy officer serves as the senior official responsible for:

- Developing, promoting, and supporting the organization's privacy programs;
- Encouraging awareness of potential privacy issues and policies; and
- Reviewing and implementing privacy regulations and legislation.

Physical Security Officer or other designated official with physical security responsibilities. The physical security officer is responsible for the overall implementation and management of physical security controls across an organization, to include integration with applicable information security controls. As information security programs are developed, senior agency officials should work to ensure this coordination of complementary controls. In consideration of information security, the physical security officer serves as the senior official responsible for:

- Developing, promulgating, implementing, and monitoring the organization's physical security programs, to include appropriate controls for alternate work sites;

- Ensuring organizational implementation and monitoring of access controls (i.e., authorization, access, visitor control, transmission medium, display medium, logging)

- Coordinating organizational environmental controls (i.e., ongoing and emergency power support and backups, fire protection, temperature and humidity controls, water damage); and

- Overseeing and managing controls for delivery and removal of assets.

Personnel Security Officer or other designated official with personnel security responsibilities. This responsibility is often resident within the Human Resources or Human Capital organization. The personnel security officer is responsible for the overall implementation and management of personnel security controls across an organization, to include integration with specific information security controls. As information security programs are developed, senior agency officials should work to ensure this coordination of complementary controls. In consideration of information security, the personnel security officer serves as the senior official responsible for:

- Developing, promulgating, implementing, and monitoring the organization's personnel security programs;

- Developing and implementing position categorization (including third-party controls), access agreements, and personnel screening, termination, and transfers; and

- Ensuring consistent and appropriate sanctions for personnel violating management, operation, or technical information security controls.

Acquisitions/Contracting. The Acquisitions/Contracting function is responsible for managing contracts and overseeing their implementation. Personnel executing this function have the following responsibilities in regards to information security:

- Collaborating with the agency's SAISO or other appropriate official to ensure that the agency's contracting policies adequately address the agency's information security requirements;

- Coordinating with the SAISO or other appropriate official as required to ensure that all agency contracts and procurements are compliant with the agency's information security policy;

- Ensuring that all personnel with responsibilities in the agency's procurement process are properly trained in information security; and

- In concert with the SAISO, facilitating the monitoring of contract performance for compliance with the agency's information security policy.

2.2.4 Federal Enterprise Architecture (FEA)

FEA is a business-based framework for governmentwide improvement. The purpose of FEA is to facilitate cross-agency analyses and identify duplicative investments, gaps, and opportunities for collaboration within and across federal agencies.[10] FEA facilitates identification of duplicative or wasteful investments, areas where investments should be made, and where departments and agencies can collaborate to improve government operations or services.

The FEA consists of five reference models:

- The Performance Reference Model (PRM) is a common framework for performance measurement that can be applied throughout the FEA.

- The Business Reference Model (BRM) is a function-driven framework for describing the business operations of the federal government independent of the agencies.

- The Service Component Reference Model (SRM) is a business- and performance-driven functional framework that classifies service components with respect to how they support business and/or performance objectives.

- The Data and Information Reference Model (DRM) describes, at an aggregate level, the data and information that support program and business line operations.

- The Technical Reference Model (TRM) is a component-driven technical framework used to identify the standards, specifications, and technologies that support and enable the delivery of service components and capabilities.

OMB requires agencies to integrate security into their enterprise architecture development life cycle.[11] In addition to complying with OMB requirements, the integration of information security into the agency enterprise architecture efforts benefits both the agencies and the federal government:

- **Reduction of the reporting burden.** The FEA requires agencies to collect and analyze significant amounts of data. The security efforts already under way can provide information relevant to the data, technology, and performance metrics in place throughout a department, such as the information contained in FISMA quarterly and annual reports, accreditation letters, and plan of actions and milestones (POA&M).

- **Integration of security data.** Organizations should use existing information security data sources to identify data for their FEA submissions, thus allowing for a continuous and reliable transmission and roll-up of security requirements and controls from initial security certification and accreditation documentation and POA&Ms into the FEA.

- **Preservation of security requirements.** Documenting and preserving information about applicable security requirements ensures that it can be used as a part of any higher-level federal management or decision-making process. If, for example, the federal government were to try and implement a large-scale reorganization (such as creating a new department or agency), a security-aware FEA would be able to clearly outline not only the intersections of common business lines but also the corresponding security requirements. In another example, if a department were to mandate using a specific type of technological tool, the FEA would be able to highlight the security and privacy requirements for the technology as well as the requirements for the data that

---

[10] OMB, 'Federal Enterprise Architecture' (FEA), 2002.
[11] OMB, 'Office of Management and Budget Circular A-130, Appendix III,' 1996.

the tool would handle. Since the federal government has numerous IT-related efforts under way, including critical infrastructure protection (CIP) and COOP processes that seek to preserve national resources as well as the ability of departments and agencies to operate in adverse or emergency conditions, a security-enabled FEA will provide support to those other efforts while simultaneously ensuring that information is appropriately protected within these efforts.

2.2.5 Information Security Policy and Guidance

Information security policy is an aggregate of directives, rules, and practices that prescribes how an organization manages, protects, and distributes information.[12]

Information security policy is an essential component of information security governance—without the policy, governance has no substance and rules to enforce. Information security policy should be based on a combination of appropriate legislation, such as FISMA; applicable standards, such as NIST Federal Information Processing Standards (FIPS) and guidance; and internal agency requirements.

Agency information security policy should address the fundamentals of agency information security governance structure, including:

- Information security roles and responsibilities;
- Statement of security controls baseline and rules for exceeding the baseline; and
- Rules of behavior that agency users are expected to follow and minimum repercussions for noncompliance.

Supporting guidance and procedures on how to effectively implement specific controls across the enterprise should be developed to augment an agency's security policy. This subsequent guidance on information security, created by the agency, in consideration of external guidance (e.g. NIST Special Publications and OMB memoranda), should be consistent with the information security policy and may not supersede it, unless the policy itself is being modified. Agencies should ensure that their information security policy is sufficiently current to accommodate the information security environment and agency mission and operational requirements. To ensure that information security does not become obsolete, agencies should implement a policy review and revision cycle. As a part of the periodic review and the initial development of the information security policies, agencies should work to ensure that all internal security policies (i.e., physical and personnel) are sufficiently coordinated to ensure effective implementation of crosscutting and convergent security objectives, such as access control initiatives.

2.2.6 Ongoing Monitoring

An effective information security governance program requires constant review. Agencies should monitor the status of their programs to ensure that:

- Ongoing information security activities are providing appropriate support to the agency mission;

- Policies and procedures are current and aligned with evolving technologies, if appropriate; and

- Controls are accomplishing their intended purpose.

---

[12] NIST SP 800-53, Revision 1, 'Recommended Security Controls for Federal Information Systems,' 2006.

Over time, policies and procedures may become inadequate because of changes in agency mission and operational requirements, threats, environment, deterioration in the degree of compliance, changes in technology or infrastructure, or business processes. Periodic assessments and reports on activities can be a valuable means of identifying areas of noncompliance, reminding users of their responsibilities and demonstrating management's commitment to the security program. While an organization's mission does not frequently change, the agency may expand its mission to secure agency programs and assets and, by extension, require modification to its information security requirements and practices. It is important that a change in an organization's internal requirements is checked against external federal requirements as, for example, a change to an information system's security posture may alter its subsequent reporting requirements.

To facilitate ongoing monitoring, the SAISO and other officials can compare and correlate a variety of real-time and static information available from a number of ongoing activities within and outside of their programs. FISMA requires agencies to perform an annual assessment of their information security programs and report information security performance measures quarterly and annually. The intent of these reporting requirements is to facilitate close to real-time assessment and monitoring of information security program activities. Ongoing monitoring combines the use of existing data to oversee a security program, and typically occurs throughout all phases of the program life cycle. Agencies can use a variety of data originating from the ongoing information security program activities to monitor performance of programs under their purview, including POA&Ms, performance measurements and metrics, continuous assessment, configuration management and control, network monitoring, and incident statistics.

Table 2-1 provides a broad overview of key ongoing activities that can assist in monitoring and improving an agency's information governance activities.

Table 2-1. Ongoing Monitoring Activities

Activities	Description of Activities	Supporting Processes and Information
Plans of Action and Milestones (POA&M)[13]	POA&Ms assist in identifying, assessing, prioritizing, and monitoring the progress of corrective efforts for security weaknesses found in programs and systems. The POA&M tracks the measures implemented to correct deficiencies and to reduce or eliminate known vulnerabilities. POA&Ms can also assist in identifying performance gaps, evaluating an agency's security performance and efficiency, and conducting oversight.	▪ Agency maintains separate program and system POA&Ms. ▪ Weaknesses are listed according to OMB criteria, identified in annual OMB FISMA guidance. ▪ System POA&Ms are tied to capital planning documents. ▪ Number of ongoing POA&M actions is either constant or is increasing, while the number of completed POA&M actions is increasing and the number of delayed POA&M actions is decreasing. ▪ Weaknesses do not reappear on the POA&M after being rectified and marked *complete*. ▪ Managers use POA&Ms for their respective systems and programs as management tools for weakness mitigation. ▪ POA&M is updated as weaknesses are closed and discovered, and therefore reflects the latest weakness mitigation status for the agency. ▪ POA&M can be easily provided to appropriate parties (OMB, IG, GAO) on demand at any point in time. ▪ A POA&M summary synopsizing agency POA&M progress is required to be submitted to OMB quarterly.

---

[13] See NIST SP 800-37, *Guide for the Security Certification and Accreditation of Federal Information Systems*, and Chapter 11, Certification, Accreditation and Security Assessments, of this guide for additional guidance on the POA&M process.

Activities	Description of Activities	Supporting Processes and Information
Measurement and Metrics[14]	Metrics are tools designed to improve performance and accountability through the collection, analysis, and reporting of relevant performance-related data. Information security metrics monitor the accomplishment of goals and objectives by quantifying the implementation level of security controls and the efficiency and effectiveness of the controls, by analyzing the adequacy of security activities, and by identifying possible improvement actions.	▪ Metrics/performance measures are aligned to the agency strategy and information security strategy, and therefore are aligned to mission requirements. ▪ Agency uses metrics/performance measures to quantify and assess its information security performance and to identify and target corrective actions. ▪ Agency decision makers use metrics/performance measures as an input into decision making regarding prioritization of activities and resource and funding allocations. ▪ Agency uses metrics/performance measures that can be obtained without spending extraordinary resources. ▪ Metrics/performance measures provide numerical and empirical data rather than opinions. ▪ Metrics/performance measures are regularly verified by third-party reviewers for accuracy and validity. ▪ Metrics/performance measures provide meaningful data to assess the impact of changes over time. ▪ Agency collects data to calculate metrics/performance measures at the most discrete, unanalyzed level possible. ▪ Agency uses well-defined and specified metrics/performance measures.
Continuous Assessment[15]	The continuous assessment process monitors the initial security accreditation of an information system to track the changes to the information system, analyzes the security impact of those changes, makes appropriate adjustments to the security controls and to the system's security plan, and reports the security status of the system to appropriate agency officials.	▪ Many agency information systems are certified and accredited more frequently than every three years. ▪ System security plans are updated frequently, as system changes occur. ▪ Results of continuous assessment process can be tracked throughout system POA&Ms. ▪ Appropriate agency officials are aware of the status of systems under their purview. ▪ System control assessments and security assessment and evaluation occur at least annually.
Configuration Management[16]	Configuration management (CM) is an essential component of monitoring the status of security controls and identifying potential security-related problems in information systems. This information can help security managers understand and monitor the evolving nature of vulnerabilities as they appear in a system under their responsibility, thus enabling managers to direct appropriate changes as required.	▪ Agency deploys a Configuration Control Board (CCB) or a similar body. ▪ An information security representative participates in the CCB. ▪ Vendor patches are tested for impact to information security and system settings. ▪ Agencies observe a decrease in incidents caused by known vulnerabilities for which patches have been distributed to system administrators. ▪ Known vulnerabilities are rarely discovered during various assessments. ▪ Staff who are responsible for CM receive appropriate information security training and are aware of their security-related responsibilities. ▪ Agency drafts and publishes standardized configuration policies, and tracks the number and frequency of implementations of configurations throughout its organization.

---

[14] See NIST SP 800-55, *Security Metrics Guide for Information Technology Systems* and Chapter 7, Performance Measures, of this guide for additional guidance on measurements and metrics.

[15] See NIST SP 800-30, *Risk Management Guide for Information Technology Systems*, Chapter 10, Risk Management, and Chapter 11, Certification, Accreditation, and Security Assessments, of this guide, for additional guidance on continuous assessment.

[16] See Chapter 14, Configuration Management, of this guide for additional guidance on configuration management.

Activities	Description of Activities	Supporting Processes and Information
Network Monitoring[17]	Information about network performance and user behavior on the network will help security program managers identify areas in need of improvement as well as point out potential performance improvements. This information can be correlated with other sources of information, such as POA&M and CM, to create a comprehensive picture of security program status.	• Network monitoring information is summarized and provided to information security program managers. • Network monitoring information is mined for trends and correlated with other data sources, including incident statistics, POA&M, CM, and other available sources. • Information security managers and system owners are able to receive and use network monitoring information to assess security posture of systems under their purview.
Incident and Event Statistics[18]	Incident statistics are valuable in determining the effectiveness of security policies and procedures implementation. Incident statistics provide security program managers with further insights into the status of security programs under their purview, observe program activities performance trends, and inform program managers about the needs to change policies and procedures.	• Agency collects incident statistics in such a manner that they can be used for regular data mining and information trending and for improving incident handling and response processes. • Incident statistical information is summarized and provided to information security program managers. • Incident statistics are mined for trends and correlated with other data sources, including network monitoring, POA&M, CM, training and awareness, and other available sources. • Information security managers and system owners are able to receive and use incident statistics to assess security posture of systems under their purview.

2.3 Information Security Governance Challenges and Keys to Success

There are many diverse, and sometimes conflicting, priorities an organization must account for in meeting information security governance requirements. These criteria present challenges an organization is likely to face in its efforts to establish information security governance.

Some of the most common challenges include:

- **Balancing extensive requirements originating from multiple governing bodies.** Several different governing and oversight bodies establish governance and information security requirements for the federal government. While these requirements are seldom contradictory, they are not always complementary, and organizations may be faced with the challenge of implementing different compliance measures and monitoring these measures for reporting purposes.

- **Balancing legislation and agency-specific policy.** Agencies may have more stringent requirements that go beyond those required by information security legislation, regulation, and directives.

- **Maintaining currency.** Governance standards and guidance evolve to support different requirements, and new legislation is frequently introduced.

- **Prioritizing available funding according to requirements.** Increased competition for limited federal budgets and resources requires that agencies allocate available funding toward their highest-priority information security investments.

Information security governance provides a framework for establishing and maintaining an information security program that will evolve with the organization it

---

[17] See NIST 800-42, Guidelines on Network Security Testing, for additional guidance on network monitoring.

[18] See NIST SP 800-61, *Computer Security Incident Handling Guide*, and Chapter 13, Incident Response, of this guide for additional guidance on incident and event statistics.

supports. The following list is a summary of good information security governance practices that are critical for ensuring the security of enterprise information assets:

- Information security activities should be governed based on relevant requirements, including laws, regulations, and organizational policies.

- Senior managers should be actively involved in establishing information security governance framework and the act of governing the agency's implementation of information security.

- Information security responsibilities must be assigned and carried out by appropriately trained individuals.

- Individuals responsible for information security within the agency should be held accountable for their actions or lack of actions.

- Information security priorities should be communicated to stakeholders of all levels within an organization to ensure a successful implementation of an information security program.

- Information security activities must be integrated into other management activities of the enterprise, including strategic planning, capital planning, and enterprise architecture.

- Information security organization structure should be appropriate for the organization it supports and should evolve with the organization, if the organization undergoes change.

- Information security managers should continuously monitor the performance of the security program/effort for which they are responsible, using available tools and information.

- Information discovered through monitoring should be used as an input into management decisions about priorities and funding allocation to effect the improvement of security posture and the overall performance of the organization.

Websites:

www.csrc.nist.gov

www.gao.gov

www.whitehouse.gov/omb/

References:

Public Law 107-347 [H.R. 2458], *The E-Government Act of 2002, Title III of this Act is the Federal Information Security Management Act of 2002 (FISMA)*, December 17, 2002.

Office of Management and Budget Circular A-130, *Management of Federal Information Resources*, November 2000.

Chapter 3

3. System Development Life Cycle

The system development life cycle (SDLC) is the overall process of developing, implementing, and retiring information systems through a multistep process from initiation, analysis, design, implementation, and maintenance to disposal. There are many different SDLC models and methodologies, but each generally consists of a series of defined steps or phases.

Various SDLC methodologies have been developed to guide the processes involved, and some methods work better than others for specific types of projects. Regardless of the type of the life cycle used by an organization, information security must be integrated into the SDLC to ensure appropriate protection for the information that the system is intended to transmit, process, and store. Security is most useful and cost-effective when such integration begins with a system development or integration project initiation, and is continued throughout the SDLC through system disposal. A number of federal laws and directives require integrating security into the SDLC, including the Federal Information Security Management Act (FISMA) and Office of Management and Budget (OMB) Circular A-130, Appendix III.

This section provides a general overview of security integration into the SDLC and is not intended to prescribe any particular model or methodology. Each phase of the SDLC includes a minimum set of information security-related activities required to effectively incorporate security into a system. An organization can either use a generic SDLC as described in this section or develop a tailored SDLC that meets its specific needs. National Institute of Standards and Technology (NIST) Special Publication (SP) 800-64 Rev. 1, *Security Considerations in the Information System Development Life Cycle*, presents a framework for incorporating security into all phases of the SDLC, depicted in Figure 3-1, to ensure the selection, acquisition, and use of appropriate and cost-effective security controls.[19]

3.1 Initiation Phase

All information technology (IT) projects have a starting point, what is commonly referred to as the initiation phase. During the initiation phase, the organization establishes the need for a particular system and documents its purpose. The information to be processed, transmitted, or stored is typically evaluated, as well as who is required access to such information and how (in high-level terms). In addition, it is often determined whether the project will be an independent information system or a component of an already-defined system. A preliminary risk assessment is typically conducted in this phase, and security planning documents are initiated (system security plan).

---

[19] See NIST Federal Information Processing Standard (FIPS) 199, *Standards for Security Categorization of Federal Information and Information Systems; NIST SP 800-60, Guide for Mapping Types of Information and Information Systems to Security Categories;* and NIST 800-37, (*Guide for the Security Certification and Accreditation of Federal Information Systems*); for additional guidance on security and the SDLC process.

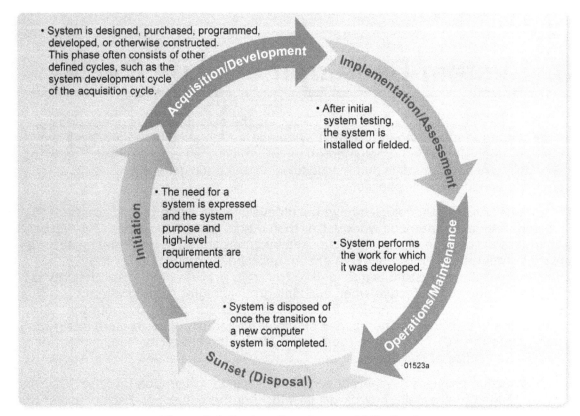

Figure 3-1. System Development Life Cycle

Once these tasks have been completed and a need has been recognized for a new or enhanced IT product or service, several processes must take place before the project is approved, to include clearly defining project goals and defining high-level information security requirements. Typically, during this phase, the organization defines high-level information security policy requirements as well as the enterprise security system architecture.

3.2 Development/Acquisition Phase

During this phase, the system is designed, purchased, programmed, developed, or otherwise constructed. This phase often consists of other defined cycles, such as the system development cycle or the acquisition cycle.

During the first part of the development/acquisition phase, the organization should simultaneously define the system's security and functional requirements. These requirements can be expressed as technical features (e.g., access control), assurances (e.g., background checks for system developers), or operational practices (e.g., awareness and training). During the last part of this phase, the organization should perform developmental testing of the technical and security features/functions to ensure that they perform as intended prior to launching the implementation and integration phase.

3.3 Implementation Phase

In the implementation phase, the organization configures and enables system security features, tests the functionality of these features, installs or implements the system, and finally, obtains a formal authorization to operate the system. Design reviews and system tests should be performed before placing the system into operation to ensure that it meets all required security specifications. In addition, if new controls are added to the application or the support system, additional acceptance tests of those new controls must be performed. This approach ensures that new controls meet security specifications and do not conflict with or invalidate existing controls. The results of the design reviews and system tests should be fully documented, updated as new reviews or tests are performed, and maintained in the official organization records.

3.4 Operations/Maintenance Phase

An effective security program demands comprehensive and continuous understanding of program and system weaknesses. In the operation and maintenance phase, systems and products are in place and operating, enhancements and/or modifications to the system are developed and tested, and hardware and/or software is added or replaced. During this phase, the organization should continuously monitor performance of the system to ensure that it is consistent with preestablished user and security requirements, and needed system modifications are incorporated.

For configuration management (CM) and control, it is important to document the proposed or actual changes in the security plan of the system. Information systems are typically in a constant state of evolution with upgrades to hardware, software, firmware, and possible modifications to the surrounding environment where the system resides. Documenting information system changes and assessing the potential impact of these changes on the security of a system is an essential part of continuous monitoring, and key to avoiding a lapse in the system security accreditation.[20]

Monitoring security controls helps to identify potential security-related problems in the information system that are not identified during the security impact analysis, which is conducted as part of the CM and control process.

3.5 Disposal Phase

The disposal phase of the system life cycle refers to the process of preserving (if applicable) and discarding system information, hardware, and software. This step is extremely important because during this phase, information, hardware, and software are moved to another system, archived, discarded, or destroyed. If performed improperly, the disposal phase can result in the unauthorized disclosure of sensitive data. When archiving information, organizations should consider the need and methods for future retrieval. While electronic information is relatively easy to store and retrieve, problems can arise if the technology used to create the records is no longer available in the future as a result of obsolescence or incompatibility with new technologies. Additionally, the organization should consider what measures must be taken for the future use of data that has been encrypted, such as taking appropriate steps to ensure the secure long-term storage of cryptographic keys. It is equally important to consider legal requirements for records retention when disposing of information systems. For federal systems, system management officials should consult with their office responsible for retaining and archiving federal records.

The removal of information from a storage medium, such as a hard disk or tape, is called sanitization. There are four categories of media sanitization: disposal,

---

[20] See Chapter 14, Configuration Management, of this guide for additional guidance on configuration management.

clearing, purging, and destroying.[21] Because different kinds of sanitization provide different levels of information protection, organizations should use information security requirements as a guide for selecting the sanitization method that best suits their needs.

3.6 Security Activities within the SDLC

Security activities must be integrated into the SDLC to ensure proper identification, design, integration, and maintenance of applicable security controls throughout an information system's life cycle as summarized in Table 3-1.

Table 3-1. Security Activities in the SDLC

SDLC Activities	Security Activities and Definitions
A. Initiation Phase	
Needs Determination	• Define a problem that might be solved through product acquisition. Traditional components of needs determination are establishing a basic system idea, defining preliminary requirements, assessing feasibility, assessing technology, and identifying a form of approval to further investigate the problem. • Establish and document need and purpose of the system.
Security Categorization	• Identify information that will be transmitted, processed, or stored by the system and define applicable levels of information categorization according to NIST SP 800-60 and FIPS 199.[22] The handling and safeguarding of personally identifiable information should be considered.
Preliminary Risk Assessment[23]	• Establish an initial description of the basic security needs of the system. A preliminary risk assessment should define the threat environment in which the system or product will operate.
B. Development/Acquisition Phase	
Requirements Analysis/ Development	• Conduct a more in-depth study of the need that draws on and further develops the work performed during the initiation phase. • Develop and incorporate security requirements into specifications. • Analyze functional requirements that may include system security environment (e.g., enterprise information security policy and enterprise security architecture) and security functional requirements. • Analyze assurance requirements that address the acquisition and product integration activities required and assurance evidence needed to produce the desired level of confidence that the product will provide required information security features correctly and effectively. The analysis, based on legal, regulatory, protection, and functional security requirements, will be used as the basis for determining how much and what kinds of assurance are required.
Risk Assessment[24]	• Conduct formal risk assessment to identify system protection requirements. This analysis builds on the initial risk assessment performed during the initiation phase, but will be more in-depth and specific. Security categories derived from FIPS 199 are typically considered during the risk assessment process to help guide the initial selection of security controls for an information system.

---

[21] See NIST SP 800-88, *Guidelines for Media Sanitization,* for additional guidance on media sanitization.

[22] NIST SP 800-60, *Guide for Mapping Types of Information and Information Systems to Security Categories;* FIPS 199, *Standards for Security Categorization of Federal Information and Information Systems.*

[23] See FIPS 199, and Chapter 10, Risk Management, and Chapter 11, Certification, Accreditation, and Security Assessments, of this guide for additional guidance on preliminary risk assessments.

[24] See NIST SP 800-30, *Risk Management Guide for Information Technology Systems;* Chapter 10, Risk Management; and Chapter 11, Certification, Accreditation, and Security Assessments, of this guide for additional guidance on risk assessments.

Cost Considerations and Reporting[25]	▪ Determine how much of the product acquisition and integration cost can be attributed to information security over the life cycle of the system. These costs include hardware, software, personnel, and training.
Security Planning[26]	▪ Fully document agreed-upon security controls, planned or in place. ▪ Develop the system security plan. ▪ Develop documents supporting the agency's information security program (e.g., CM plan, contingency plan, incident response plan, security awareness and training plan, rules of behavior, risk assessment, security test and evaluation results, system interconnection agreements, security authorizations/accreditations, and plans of action and milestones [POA&M]). ▪ Develop awareness and training requirements, including user manuals and operations/administrative manuals.
Security Control Development[27]	▪ Develop, design, and implement security controls described in the respective security plans. For information systems currently in operation, the security plans for those systems that may call for developing additional security controls to supplement the controls already in place or for those that may call for modifying selected controls that are deemed to be less than effective.
Developmental Security Test and Evaluation	▪ Test security controls developed for a new information system or product for proper and effective operation. Some types of security controls (primarily those controls of a nontechnical nature) cannot be tested and evaluated until the information system is deployed; these controls are typically management and operational controls. ▪ Develop test plan/script/scenarios.
Other Planning Components	▪ Ensure that all necessary components of the product acquisition and integration process are considered when incorporating security into the life cycle. These components include selection of the appropriate contract type, participation by all necessary functional groups within an organization, participation by the certifier and accreditor, and development and execution of necessary contracting plans and processes.
C. Implementation Phase	
Security Test and Evaluation	▪ Develop test data. ▪ Test unit, subsystem, and entire system. ▪ Ensure system undergoes technical evaluation (e.g., according to federal laws [Sec. 508], regulations, policies, guidelines, and standards).
Inspection and Acceptance	▪ Verify and validate that the functionality described in the specification is included in the deliverables.
System Integration/ Installation	▪ Integrate the system at the operational site where it is to be deployed for operation. Enable security control settings and switches in accordance with vendor instructions and proper security implementation guidance.
Security Certification[28]	▪ Ensure that the controls are effectively implemented through established verification techniques and procedures and give organization officials confidence that the appropriate safeguards and countermeasures are in place to protect the organization's information. Security certification also uncovers and describes the known vulnerabilities in the information system. Existing security certification may need to be updated to include acquired products. NIST SP 800-37 states that security certification determines the extent to which the security controls in the information system are implemented correctly, operating as intended, and producing the desired outcome with respect to meeting security requirements for the system.

---

[25] See NIST SP 800-65, *Integrating Security into the Capital Planning Process and Investment and Control Process,* and Chapter 5, Capital Planning, of this guide for additional guidance on cost considerations and reporting.

[26] See NIST SP 800-18, *Guide for Developing Security Plans for Federal Information Systems Revision 1,* NIST SP 800-65, *Integrating Security into the Capital Planning Process and Investment and Control Process,* and Chapter 5, Capital Planning, of this guide for additional guidance on cost considerations and reporting, and Chapter 8, Security Planning, of this guide for additional guidance on security planning.

[27] See NIST FIPS 200, *Minimum Security Requirements for Federal Information and Information Systems,* and NIST SP 800-53, *Recommended Security Controls for Federal Information Systems,* for additional guidance on security control development.

Security Accreditation[29]	▪ Provide the necessary security authorization of an information system to process, store, or transmit information that is required. This authorization is granted by a senior organization official and is based on the verified effectiveness of security controls to some agreed-upon level of assurance and on an identified residual risk to agency assets or operations. This process determines whether the remaining known vulnerabilities in the information system pose an acceptable level of risk to agency operations, agency assets, or individuals. Upon successful completion of this phase, system owners will either have authority to operate, interim authorization to operate, or denial of authorization to operate the information system.
D. Operations/Maintenance Phase	
Configuration Management and Control[30]	▪ Ensure adequate consideration of the potential security impacts due to specific changes to an information system or its surrounding environment. CM and configuration control procedures are critical to establishing an initial baseline of hardware, software, and firmware components for the information system and for subsequently controlling and maintaining an accurate inventory of any changes to the system. ▪ Develop CM plan 　– Establish baselines 　– Identify configuration 　– Describe configuration control process 　– Identify schedule for configuration audits
Continuous Monitoring	▪ Monitor security controls to ensure that controls continue to be effective in their application through periodic testing and evaluation. Security control monitoring (i.e., verifying the continued effectiveness of those controls over time) and reporting the security status of the information system to appropriate agency officials is an essential activity of a comprehensive information security program. Monitor to ensure system security controls are functioning as required. ▪ Perform self-administered or independent security audits or other assessments periodically. Types: using automated tools, internal control audits, security checklists, and penetration testing. ▪ Monitor system and/or users. Methods: review system logs and reports, use automated tools, review change management, monitor external sources (trade literature, publications, electronic news, etc.), and perform periodic reaccreditation. 　– POA&Ms 　– Measurement and metrics 　– Network monitoring
E. Disposal Phase:	
Information Preservation	▪ Retain information, as necessary, to conform to current legal requirements and to accommodate future technology changes that may render the retrieval method obsolete. ▪ Consult with agency office on retaining and archiving federal records. ▪ Ensure long-term storage of cryptographic keys for encrypted data. ▪ Determine archive, discard or destroy information.
Media Sanitization	▪ Determine sanitization level (overwrite, degauss, or destroy). ▪ Delete, erase, and overwrite data as necessary.
Hardware and Software Disposal	▪ Dispose of hardware and software as directed by governing agency policy.

Website:

www.csrc.nist.gov

---

[28] See NIST SP 800-37, *Guide for the Security Certification and Accreditation of Federal Information Systems*, and Chapter 11, Certification, Accreditation, and Security Assessments of this guide for additional guidance on security certification.

[29] See NIST SP 800-37, *Guide for the Security Certification and Accreditation of Federal Information Systems,* and Chapter 11, Certification, Accreditation, and Security Assessments of this guide for additional guidance on security accreditation.

[30] See Chapter 14, Configuration Management, of this guide for additional guidance on configuration management and control.

References:

Public Law 107-347 [H.R. 2458], *The E-Government Act of 2002, Title III of this Act is the Federal Information Security Management Act of 2002 (FISMA)*, December 17, 2002.

Office of Management and Budget Circular A-130, *Management of Federal Information Resources*, November 2000.

Federal Information Processing Standard 199, *Standards for Security Categorization of Federal Information and Information Systems*, February 2004.

Federal Information Processing Standard 200, *Minimum Security Requirements for Federal Information and Information Systems*, March 2006.

National Institute of Standards and Technology Special Publication 800-18 Revision 1, *Guide for Developing Security Plans for Federal Information Systems*, February 2006.

National Institute of Standards and Technology Special Publication 800-30, *Risk Management Guide for Information Technology Systems*, July 2002.

National Institute of Standards and Technology Special Publication 800-37, *Guide for the Security Certification and Accreditation of Federal Information System*, May 2004.

National Institute of Standards and Technology Special Publication 800-53, *Recommended Security Controls for Federal Information Systems*, February 2005.

National Institute of Standards and Technology Special Publication 800-60, *Guide for Mapping Types of Information and Information Systems to Security Categories*, June 2004.

National Institute of Standards and Technology Special Publication 800-64, *Security Considerations in the Information System Development Life Cycle*, Rev. 1, June 2004.

National Institute of Standards and Technology Special Publication 800-65, *Integrating Security into the Capital Planning and Investment Control Process*, January 2005.

National Institute of Standards and Technology Special Publication 800-88, *Guidelines for Media Sanitization*, September 2006.

Chapter 4

4. Awareness and Training

The security awareness and training program is a critical component of the information security program. It is *the* vehicle for disseminating security information that the workforce, including managers, need to do their jobs. In terms of the total security solution, the importance of the workforce in achieving information security goals and the importance of training as a countermeasure cannot be overstated. Establishing and maintaining a robust and relevant information security awareness and training program as part of the overall information security program is the primary conduit for providing the workforce with the information and tools needed to protect an agency's vital information resources. These programs will ensure that personnel at all levels of the organization understand their information security responsibilities to properly use and protect the information and resources entrusted to them. Agencies that continually train their workforce in organizational security policy and role-based security responsibilities will have a higher rate of success in protecting information.

As cited in audit reports, periodicals, and conference presentations, people are arguably the weakest element in the security formula that is used to secure systems and networks. The *people factor*, not technology, is a critical factor that is often overlooked in the security equation. It is for this reason that the Federal Information Security Management Act (FISMA) and the Office of Personnel Management (OPM) have mandated that more and better attention must be devoted to awareness activities and role-based training, as they are the only security controls that can minimize the inherent risk that results from the people who use, manage, operate, and maintain information systems and networks.[31] Robust and enterprise-wide awareness and training programs are needed to address this growing concern.

National Institute of Standards and Technology (NIST) Special Publication (SP) 800-50, *Building an Information Technology Security Awareness and Training Program*, provides guidelines that can help federal departments and agencies meet their information security awareness and training responsibilities defined in FISMA and in Office of Management and Budget (OMB) policy. The publication identifies models for building and maintaining a comprehensive awareness and training program as part of an organization's information security program.

NIST SP 800-50 is a companion publication to NIST SP 800-16, *Information Technology Security Training Requirements: A Role- and Performance-Based Model*. NIST SP 800-50 works at a higher strategic level and discusses how to build and maintain an information security awareness and training program; NIST SP 800-16 addresses a more tactical level and discusses the awareness-training-education continuum, role-based training, and course content considerations. The learning continuum is shown in Figure 4-1.

---

[31] Office of Personnel Management (OPM), 5 Code of Federal Regulations (CFR), Subpart C, Section 930, 301.

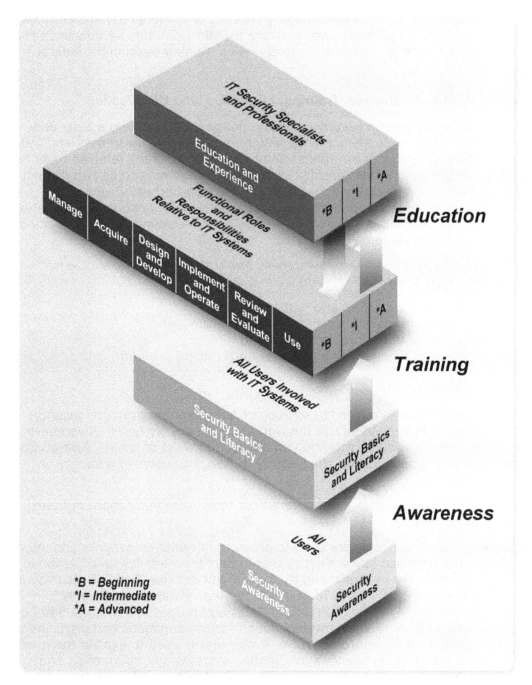

Figure 4-1. The IT Security Learning Continuum

4.1 Awareness and Training Policy

All users have information security responsibilities. FISMA mandates that all users complete "awareness training," though NIST publications call this "awareness." FISMA also tasks agencies with identifying and training those individuals who have significant responsibilities for information security, a requirement formalized by OPM's information security awareness and training policy promulgated in June 2004. OPM's policy strengthens the FISMA requirement for user exposure to "awareness training" by adding "at least annually," and requires agencies to provide "role-specific training" in accordance with NIST guidance. Although there is no federal mandate for formal education (provided by colleges or universities) and certification of information security professionals, they are mentioned in this section since some agencies include them as part of a comprehensive training solution for federal employees.

4.2 Components: Awareness, Training, Education, and Certification

An agency's information security program policy should contain a clear and distinct section devoted to agency-wide requirements for the awareness and training program. Although security awareness and training is generally referred to as "a" program, many organizations consider awareness and training to be two distinct functions, each with separate purposes, goals, and approaches. Proper implementation of these components (with consideration of options like education and professional certification) promotes professional development, which leads to a high-performance workforce.

Requirements for the security awareness and training program should be documented in the enterprise-level policy and should include:

- Definition of security roles and responsibilities;
- Development of program strategy and a program plan;
- Implementation of the program plan; and
- Maintenance of the security awareness and training program.[32]

4.2.1 Awareness

Security awareness is a blended solution of activities that promote security, establish accountability, and inform the workforce of security news. Awareness seeks to focus an individual's attention on an issue or a set of issues. Awareness is a program that continually pushes the security message to users in a variety of formats.

An awareness program includes a variety of tools, communication, outreach, and metrics development.

- **Tools.** Awareness tools are used to promote information security and inform users of threats and vulnerabilities that impact their agency and "personal" work environment by explaining the "what" but not the "how" of security, and communicating what is and what is not allowed. Awareness not only communicates information security policies and procedures that need to be followed, but also provides the foundation for any sanctions and disciplinary actions imposed for noncompliance. Awareness is used to explain the rules of behavior for using an agency's information systems and information and establishes a level of expectation on the acceptable use of the information and information systems. Types of tools include:

  - Events, such as a security awareness day;
  - Promotional materials;
  - Briefings (program- or system-specific- or issue-specific); and
  - Rules of behavior.

- **Communication.** A large part of an awareness effort is communication with users, managers, executives, system owners, and others. A communications

---

[32] NIST SP 800-50, *Building an Information Technology Security Awareness and Training Program*, October 2003.

plan is needed to identify stakeholders, types of information that is to be disseminated, channels for disseminating information, and the frequency of information exchanges. The plan also identifies whether the communications are one-way or two-way. Activities that support communication include:

- Assessment (as is/to be models);
- Strategic plan; and
- Program implementation.

- **Outreach.** Outreach is critical for leveraging best practices within the federal sector. It has two elements for intra- and interagency awareness. The intra-agency element promotes internal awareness of information security. A Web portal that provides a one-stop-shop for security information can be an effective outreach tool. Policy, frequently asked questions (FAQs), security e-newsletters, links to resources, and other useful information are easily accessible to all employees. This tool promotes a consistent and standard message. The interagency element promotes sharing among agencies and is used to leverage awareness and training resources.

4.2.2 Training

Information security training strives to produce relevant and needed security knowledge and skills within the workforce. Training supports competency development and helps personnel understand and learn how to perform their security role. The most important difference between training and awareness is that training seeks to teach skills that allow a person to perform a specific function, while awareness seeks to focus an individual's attention on an issue or a set of issues.

Role-based training provides security courses that are tailored to the specific needs of each group of people who have been identified as having significant responsibilities for information security in their organization. NIST SP 800-16 provides guidance for establishing role- and performance-based security training programs.

4.2.3 Education

Education integrates all of the security skills and competencies of the various functional specialties into a common body of knowledge and adds a multidisciplinary study of concepts, issues, and principles (technological and social). Information security education strives to produce information security specialists and professionals who are capable of vision and proactive response. Several colleges and universities provide academic programs to support the information security needs of the public and private sectors. Many of these schools partner with the federal sector to accomplish research and development tasks to improve information security.

4.2.4 Certification

In response to the growing demand for information security personnel within federal agencies, there has been a movement toward increased professional standards for federal and contracted security personnel. This "professionalization" integrates training, education, and experience with an assessment mechanism to validate knowledge and skills, resulting in the "certification" of a predefined level of competence. The relationship among these professional development elements is illustrated in Figure 4-2.

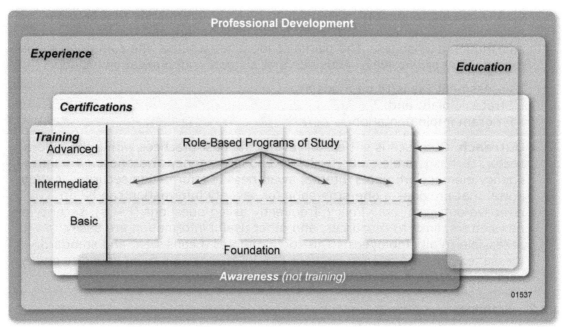

Figure 4-2. Elements of Professional Development

It should be noted that there are distinct differences among certifications that are offered by a variety of organizations. Primarily, one will encounter certificates of completion, certifications awarded by an industry and/or vendors, and graduate-level certificates awarded by academic institutions:

- **Certificates of completion** are provided to individuals solely as a testament to completion of a particular course—these certificates do not make any claims that the individual actually gained knowledge and/or skills.

- **Industry and/or vendor certification** requires a combination of training, education, and experience. These certifications validate knowledge and skills through testing—they provide varying degrees of assurance that an individual has a baseline level of knowledge, skills, and abilities (KSAs) with regard to a predefined body of knowledge. The preparatory work for knowledge-based or skill-based certifications normally includes training in a prescribed body of knowledge or technical curriculum and is supplemented frequently by on-the-job experience.

- **Graduate certificates** in information security are awarded by an academic institution to individuals who successfully complete all graduation requirements for a particular program. These graduate certificates generally require 18 to 21 credit hours of academic study, have at least four required courses, allow for one or two electives, and may require some form of research paper, project, or case study.

4.3 Designing, Developing, and Implementing an Awareness and Training Program

The development of an information security awareness and training program involves three major steps:

1. *Designing* the program (including the development of the information security awareness and training program plan);

2. *Developing* the awareness and training material; and
3. *Implementing* the program.

Even a small amount of information security awareness and training can go a long way toward improving the security posture of, and vigilance within, an organization.

4.3.1 Designing an Awareness and Training Program

Awareness and training programs must be designed with the mission of the agency in mind. The awareness and training program must support the business needs of the organization and be relevant to the organization's culture and information technology architecture. The most successful programs are those that users feel are relevant to the subject matter and issues presented.

Designing an information security awareness and training program answers the question "What is our plan for developing and implementing awareness and training opportunities that are compliant with existing directives?" In the design step of the program, the agency's awareness and training needs are identified, an effective agency-wide awareness and training plan is developed, organizational buy-in is sought and secured, and priorities are established.

4.3.2 Developing an Awareness and Training Program

Once the awareness and training program has been designed, supporting material can be developed. Material should be developed with the following in mind:

- "What behavior do we want to reinforce?" (awareness)
- "What skill or skills do we want the audience to learn and apply?" (training and education).

In both cases, the focus should be on specific material that the participants should integrate into their jobs. Attendees will pay attention and incorporate what they see or hear in a session if they feel that the material was developed specifically for them. Any presentation that feels so impersonal and general that it could be given to any audience, will be filed away as just another of the annual "we're here because we have to be here" sessions. An awareness and training program can be effective, however, if the material is interesting, current, and relevant.

The awareness audience must include all users in an organization. Users may include employees, contractors, foreign or domestic guest researchers, other agency personnel, visitors, guests, and other collaborators or associates requiring access. The message to be spread through an awareness program, or campaign, should make all individuals aware of their commonly shared information security responsibilities.

On the other hand, the message in a training class is directed at a specific audience. The message in training material should include everything related to security that attendees need to know in order to perform their jobs. Training material is usually far more in-depth than material used in an awareness session or campaign.

4.3.3 Implementing an Awareness and Training Program

An information security awareness and training program should be implemented only after a needs assessment has been conducted, a strategy has been developed, an awareness and training program plan for implementing that strategy has been completed, and awareness and training material has been developed.

The program's implementation must be fully explained to the organization to achieve support for its implementation and commitment of necessary resources. This explanation includes expectations of agency management and staff support, as well as expected results of the program and benefits to the organization. Funding issues must also be addressed. For example, agency managers must know if the cost to implement the awareness and training program will be totally funded by the chief information officer (CIO) or information security program budget, or if their budgets will be impacted to cover their share of the expense of implementing the program. It is essential that everyone involved in the implementation of the program understand their roles and responsibilities. In addition, schedules and completion requirements must be communicated.

Once the plan for implementing the awareness and training program has been explained to (and accepted by) agency management, the implementation can begin. Since there are several ways to present and disseminate awareness and training material throughout an organization, agencies should tailor their implementation to the size, organization, and complexity of their enterprise.[33]

4.4 Post-Implementation

An organization's information security awareness and training program can quickly become obsolete if sufficient attention is not paid to technology advancements, IT infrastructure changes, organizational changes, and shifts in organizational mission and priorities. CIOs and senior agency information security officers (SAISOs) need to be cognizant of this potential problem and incorporate mechanisms into their strategy to ensure that the program continues to be relevant and compliant with overall objectives. Continuous improvement should always be the theme for security awareness and training initiatives, as this is one area where *"you can never do enough."* Efforts supporting this post-implementation feedback loop should be developed in consideration of the security organization's overall ongoing performance measures program.[34]

4.4.1 Monitoring Compliance

Once the program has been implemented, processes must be put in place to monitor compliance and effectiveness. An automated tracking system should be designed to capture key information on program activity (e.g., courses, dates, audience, costs, sources). The tracking system should capture this data at an agency level, so it can be used to provide enterprise-wide analysis and reporting regarding awareness, training, and education initiatives.

Tracking compliance involves assessing the status of the program as indicated by the database information and mapping it to standards established by the agency. Reports can be generated and used to identify gaps or problems. Corrective action and necessary follow-up can then be taken. This follow-up may take the form of formal reminders to management; additional awareness, training, or education offerings; and/or the establishment of a corrective plan with scheduled completion dates.

---

[33] See NIST SP 800-50 for techniques for delivering awareness and training material.
[34] See NIST SP 800-55, *Security Metrics Guide for Information Technology Systems,* and Chapter 7, Performance Measures, of this guide for additional guidance on measurements and metrics.

4.4.2   Evaluation and Feedback

Formal evaluation and feedback mechanisms are critical components of any security awareness and training program. Continuous improvement cannot occur without a good sense of how the existing program is working. In addition, the feedback mechanism must be designed to address objectives initially established for the program. Once the baseline requirements have been solidified, a feedback strategy can be designed and implemented. Various evaluation and feedback mechanisms that can be used to update the awareness and training program plan include surveys, evaluation forms, independent observation, status reports, interviews, focus groups, technology shifts, and/or benchmarking.

A feedback strategy should incorporate elements that address quality, scope, deployment method (e.g., Web-based, onsite, offsite), level of difficulty, ease of use, duration of session, relevancy, currency, and suggestions for modification.

Metrics are essential to feedback and evaluation. They can be used to:

- Measure the effectiveness of the security awareness and training program;
- Provide information for many of the data requests that an agency must provide with regard to compliance; and,
- Provide an important gauge for demonstrating progress and identifying areas for improvement.

4.5 Managing Change

It is necessary to ensure that the program, as structured, continues to evolve as new technology and associated security issues emerge. Training needs will shift as new skills and capabilities become necessary to respond to new architectural and technology changes. A change in the organizational mission and/or objectives can also influence ideas on how best to design training solutions and content. Emerging issues, such as homeland defense, will also impact the nature and extent of security awareness and training activities necessary to keep users informed and/or trained about the latest threats, vulnerabilities, and countermeasures. New laws and court decisions may also impact agency policy that, in turn, may affect the development and/or implementation of awareness and training material. Finally, as security policies evolve, awareness and training material should reflect these changes.

4.6 Program Success Indicators

CIOs, program officials, and SAISOs should be primary advocates for awareness, training, education, and professionalization.   Securing an organization's information and infrastructure is a team effort, requiring the dedication of capable individuals to carry out their assigned security roles within the organization. Listed below are some key indicators to gauge the support for, and acceptance of, the program:

- Key stakeholder demonstrates commitment and support;
- Sufficient funding is budgeted and available to implement the agreed-upon awareness and training strategy;
- Appropriate organizational placement of senior officials with key security responsibilities (CIO, program officials, and SAISO) facilitates strategy implementation;

- Infrastructure to support broad distribution (e.g., Web, e-mail, learning management systems) and posting of security awareness and training materials is funded and implemented;
- Executive/senior-level officials deliver messages to staff regarding security (e.g., staff meetings, broadcasts to all users by agency head), champion the program, and demonstrate support for training by committing financial resources to the program;
- Metrics indicate improved security performance by the workforce (e.g., to explain a decline in security incidents or violations, indicate that the gap between existing awareness and training coverage and identified needs is shrinking, the percentage of users being exposed to awareness material is increasing, the percentage of users with significant security responsibilities being appropriately trained is increasing);
- Executives and managers do not use their status in the organization to avoid security controls that are consistently adhered to by the rank and file;
- Level of attendance at security forums/briefings/training is consistently high.
- Recognition of security contributions (e.g., awards, contests) is a standard practice within an agency; and
- Individuals playing key roles in managing/coordinating the security program demonstrate commitment to the program and motivation to promote the program.

Website:
www.csrc.nist.gov

References:

Public Law 107-347 [H.R. 2458], The E-Government Act of 2002, Title III of this Act is the Federal Information Security Management Act of 2002 (FISMA), December 17, 2002.

Office of Personnel Management, 5 Code of Federal Regulations, Subpart C, Employees Responsible for the Management or Use of Federal Computer Systems, Section 930.301, Computer Security Training Program.

National Institute of Standards and Technology Special Publication 800-16, *Information Technology Security Training Requirements: A Role- and Performance-Based Model*, April 1998.

National Institute of Standards and Technology Special Publication 800-50, *Building an Information Technology Security Awareness and Training Program*, October 2003.

National Institute of Standards and Technology Special Publication 800-55, *Security Metrics Guide for Information Technology Systems,* July 2003.

Chapter 5

5. Capital Planning and Investment Control

Increased competition for limited federal budgets and resources requires that agencies allocate available funding toward their highest-priority information security investments to afford the agency and its systems and data, the appropriate degree of security for their needs. This goal can be achieved through a formal enterprise capital planning and investment control (CPIC) process designed to facilitate and control the expenditure of agency funds. The Federal Information Security Management Act (FISMA) and other existing federal regulations charge federal agencies with integrating information security activities and the capital planning and investment control process. The practices discussed in this chapter are designed to help security practitioners and managers identify funding needs to secure systems and provide strategies for obtaining the necessary funding.

5.1 Legislative Overview

Implementation of information security within the federal government is guided by a combination of legislation, rules and regulations, and agency-specific policies. FISMA is the overarching information security legislation for federal information systems. Signed into law in 2002, FISMA:

- Charges the Office of Management and Budget (OMB) and NIST to develop security standards and identify tolerable security risk levels;
- Makes NIST standards compulsory for all agencies; FISMA eliminated an agency's ability to obtain waivers on NIST standards (Federal Information Processing Standard [FIPS]); and
- Charges agencies to integrate information security into CPIC.

- **NIST SP 800-53** identifies a set of minimum security controls applicable to information systems based on FIPS 199 categorization (low, moderate, high).

- **OMB Circular A-11** directs agencies to complete Exhibit 300s and an Exhibit 53. The Exhibit 300 reflects an investment's plan for capital asset management. The Exhibit 300 is an input to the Exhibit 53, which provides the total information technology (IT) and information security spending for the year.

- **FISMA Report** is an annual report to OMB detailing the agency's security posture and any areas of weakness.[35]

- **Plan of Action and Milestones (POA&M)** documents each agency security weakness, associated corrective action, and the corrective action cost.[36]

As Figure 5-1 illustrates, the corrective action and cost information contained in the POA&M serve as inputs to the Exhibit 300s and are then rolled into the Exhibit

---

[35] See Chapter 11, Certification, Accreditation, and Security Assessments, of this guide for additional guidance on FISMA reporting.
[36] See Chapter 11, Certification, Accreditation, and Security Assessments, of this guide for additional guidance on POA&Ms.

53. Exhibit 300s and Exhibit 53 are part of the agency's budget submission to OMB and provide an overview of an agency's IT portfolio.

To facilitate effective implementation of OMB capital planning and NIST security requirements, the Government Accountability Office (GAO) offers a Select-Control-Evaluate investment life-cycle model as a best practices approach to investment management. While not compulsory, the framework articulates key activities for managing IT investments throughout the life cycle. The three phases ensure that investment management practices, including security, are disciplined and thorough throughout each phase of the investment life cycle. Figure 5-1 illustrates the three phases.

The Select phase refers to activities involved with assessing and prioritizing current and proposed IT projects based on mission needs and improvement priorities, and then creates a portfolio of IT projects to address these needs and priorities. Typical Select phase activities include screening new projects; analyzing and ranking all projects based on benefit, cost, and risk criteria; selecting a portfolio of projects; and establishing project review schedules.

The Control phase refers to activities designated to monitor the investment during its operational phase to determine whether the investment is within the cost and schedule milestones established at the beginning of the investment life cycle. Typical processes involved in the Control phase include using a set of performance measures to monitor the developmental progress for each IT project to enable early problem identification and resolution.

The Evaluate phase refers to determining the efficacy of the investment, answering the question, "Did the investment achieve the desired results and performance goals identified during the Select phase?"

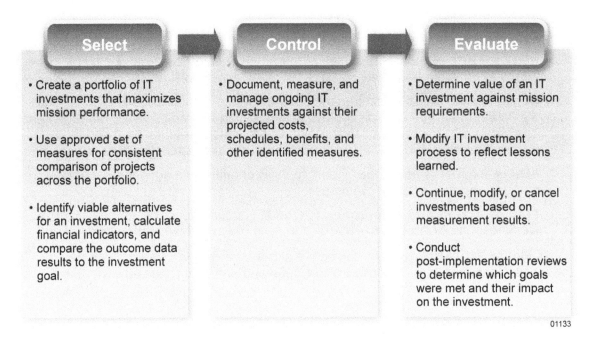

Figure 5-1. Select-Control-Evaluate Investment Life Cycle

Figure 5-1 illustrates the relationship between security drivers in the GAO Select-Control-Evaluate investment lifecycle and the System Development Life Cycle (SDLC). During the **Select** phase, security drivers include assessment activities to ensure that IT security investments comply with security requirements. During the **Control** phase, investments are monitored through the use of security metrics to ensure that security controls are in place and operational, and that investments remain compliant with requirements. During the **Evaluate** phase, security drivers include self-assessment activities to ensure compliance and media sanitization efforts following removal from operation and prior to disposition.

5.2 Integrating Information Security into the CPIC Process

National Institute of Standards and Technology (NIST) Special Publication (SP) 800-65, *Integrating IT Security into the Capital Planning and Investment Control Process*, provides a seven-step process, illustrated in Figure 5-2, for prioritizing security activities and corrective actions:

1. **Identify the Baseline:** use information security metrics or other available data to baseline the current security posture.

2. **Identify Prioritization Requirements:** evaluate security posture against legislative and chief information officer (CIO)-articulated requirements and agency mission.

3. **Conduct Enterprise-Level Prioritization:** prioritize potential enterprise-level information security investments against the mission and the financial impact of implementing appropriate security controls.

4. **Conduct System-Level Prioritization:** prioritize potential system-level corrective actions against system category and corrective action impact.

5. **Develop Supporting Materials:** for enterprise-level investments, develop concept paper, business case analysis, and Exhibit 300. For system-level investments, adjust Exhibit 300 to request additional funding to mitigate prioritized weaknesses.

Figure 5-2. Integrating Information Security into the CPIC Process

6. **Implement Investment Review Board (IRB) and Portfolio Management:** prioritize agency-wide business cases against requirements and CIO priorities and determine investment portfolio.

7. **Submit Exhibit 300s, Exhibit 53, and Conduct Program Management:** ensure approved 300s become part of the agency's Exhibit 53; ensure investments are managed through their life cycle.

The following sections provide an overview of the integration of information security into the CPIC process to help ensure that corrective actions identified in the annual FISMA reporting process through POA&Ms are incorporated into the CPIC process to deliver maximum security in a cost-effective manner.

5.3 Capital Planning and Investment Control Roles and Responsibilities[37]

Integrating information security into the CPIC process requires input and collaboration across operating units and lines of business throughout the life cycle of technology investments. Figure 5-3 depicts a hierarchical approach to the CPIC process in which investment decisions are made at both the enterprise and operating-unit levels.

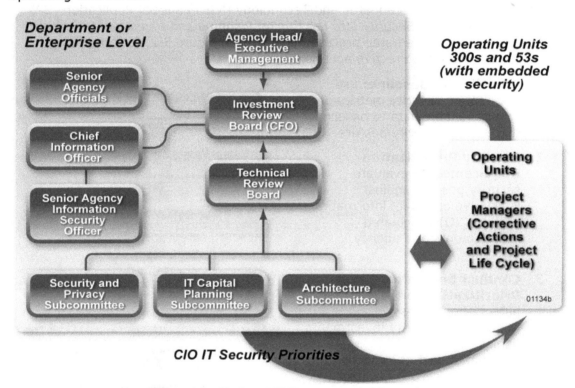

Figure 5-3. Notional IT Management Hierarchy

While specific practices for investment management can differ at the operating-unit level because of varying mission scopes, the process generally mirrors the process at the departmental level. The CIO formulates and articulates information security priorities to the organization to be considered within the context of all agency investments. Priorities may be based on agency mission and executive branch guidance such as the President's Management Agenda (PMA), OMB guidance, or other external/internal priorities. Examples of security priorities include certifying and accrediting all systems or implementing public key infrastructure (PKI) throughout the enterprise. It is important to note that OMB/executive branch guidance or laws should be ranked highest among these priorities.

Once operating units finalize their IT portfolios and budget requests for the budget year, they forward their requests to the agency-level decision makers. At the

---

[37] See Chapter 2, Information Security Governance, Chapter 8, Security Planning, Chapter 11, Certification, Accreditation, and Security Assessments, and Chapter 14, Configuration Management, of this guide for additional guidance on roles and responsibilities.

agency level, several committees evaluate IT portfolios from the operating units as referenced in Figure 5-3, culminating in a review by the IRB. The IRB then decides on an agency-level IT portfolio and forwards recommendations to the agency head for review. Once the agency-level IT portfolio is approved by the agency head, the necessary Exhibit 300s and Exhibit 53 are forwarded to OMB for funding consideration.

Many different stakeholders, from information security, capital planning, and executive leadership areas, have key roles and make decisions on integrating information security into the CPIC process with the ultimate goal of forming a well-balanced IT portfolio. Involvement at the enterprise and operating-unit levels throughout the process allows agencies to ensure that CPIC and information security goals and objectives are met. Figure 5-4 identifies typical leading, supporting, or approving roles for each stakeholder as they apply to the integration of security into the CPIC process phases.

CPIC Steps	Identify Baseline	Identify Priority Requirements	Enterprise-Level Prioritization	System-Level Prioritization	Develop Supporting Materials	Portfolio Management	Develop 53s and 300s
Agency Head		Approves				Approves	Approves
CIO, Senior Agency Information Security Officer, and Senior Agency Officials	Leads	Leads	Leads	Leads	Supports	Leads	Leads
Investment Review Board	Approves	Supports	Approves	Approves	Approves	Approves	Approves
Technical Review Board		Supports	Supports	Supports	Supports	Supports	Supports
Capital Planning, Architecture, and Security and Privacy Subcommittees	Supports	Supports	Supports	Supports	Supports	Supports	Supports
Operating Units	Supports		Leads	Leads	Leads		Leads

Legend: Approves = ☆ Leads = ▲ Supports = ●

01139c

Figure 5-4. Roles and Responsibilities throughout the CPIC Process

5.4 Identify Baseline

The first step in integrating information security and the CPIC process is to assess the security baseline. The security baseline provides a snapshot of the agency's compliance with baseline security requirements (BLSRs) and is instrumental in identifying information security strengths and weaknesses. The result of a security baseline analysis enables agency executives to evaluate their information security posture and identify areas for improvement. Agencies can identify their baselines for enterprise-level and system-level investments. System-level investments are those security investments designed to strengthen a discrete system's security posture, such as strengthening password controls or testing a contingency plan for a particular system. Enterprise-level investments are those security investments that are ubiquitous across the agency and will improve the overall agency's security posture, such as the acquisition of an enterprise-wide firewall or intrusion detection system (IDS).

NIST SP 800-55, *Security Metrics Guide for Information Technology Systems*, provides guidance on developing and implementing an information security metrics program. Metrics can provide baseline compliance percentages that indicate the existence of adequate security controls, highlight current weaknesses, and identify gaps between actual and desired implementation status of information security controls. The goal of the security baseline establishment exercise is to provide agency officials an understanding of the strengths, weaknesses, and vulnerabilities that exist within the agency's security controls and to help identify investments that are required to mitigate weaknesses. The resulting vulnerabilities and weaknesses then serve as inputs into the next step of the CPIC process: identifying prioritization criteria.

5.5 Identify Prioritization Criteria

Available funding does not always allow all security needs identified in the baseline assessment to be addressed immediately. Therefore, requirements must be prioritized to address the most pressing security investment needs first. Specific prioritization criteria will vary from agency to agency depending on specific agency mission and goals and applicable legislation and regulations. Examples of information security priorities include:

- Complying with statutory requirements in Clinger-Cohen Act, FISMA, and OMB Circular A-130 guidance;
- Implementing a risk-based security program (FISMA, Executive Orders, and supporting NIST standards and guidance); for example, implementing the security controls outlined in NIST SP 800-53;
- Safeguarding national and agency mission-critical assets (Homeland Security Presidential Directives);
- Improving information security program status; and
- Completing a security certification and accreditation of all systems in accordance with NIST SP 800-37, *Guide for the Security Certification and Accreditation of Federal Information Systems*.

A variety of taxonomies can be used to organize prioritization criteria, including FIPS 200 security control families or other agency-specific categories.

5.6 Conduct System- and Enterprise-Level Prioritization[38]

Once agency management and stakeholders agree on the prioritization of investments, the agency can begin the prioritizing process by rank-ordering requirements against the prioritization criteria. The objective of this activity is to fund first the most critical security investment. The next layer of funding should then be applied to the next critical security investment and so forth, until the security budget is entirely expended, or priorities met, whichever comes first.

Before conducting corrective action prioritization, the agency should allocate the funding necessary to mitigate significant deficiencies and other needs that obviously require attention. These initiatives should then be removed from the prioritization process to avoid duplication of effort.

After identifying the security baseline and prioritization criteria, an agency can prioritize corrective actions at two levels:

---

[38] The information presented in this special publication provides an overview of the prioritization process. For a detailed explanation of suggested system- and enterprise-level prioritization procedures, see NIST SP 800-65, pages 28-36.

1. **System-level prioritization:** prioritize corrective actions to address system-level security weaknesses and vulnerabilities found during the baseline assessment against the predefined prioritization criteria. This prioritization is performed at the operating unit level by system owners and program managers.[39]

2. **Enterprise-level prioritization:** prioritize enterprise-wide security corrective actions identified during the baseline assessment based on predefined prioritization criteria. This prioritization is performed at the enterprise level by agency information security stakeholders.

The prioritization methodology relies primarily on existing data sources and inputs. Specific data inputs for the two types of prioritization are highlighted in Table 5-1.

Table 5-1. Prioritization Data Inputs

Inputs	Source	Data Accessibility
System-Level Information		
System categorization	System security certification and accreditation, security plan or categorization according to NIST SP 800-60 and Federal Information Processing Standard (FIPS) 199.[40]	Security certification and accreditation, security plans, and NIST SP 800-60/NIST FIPS 199 categorizations are required for all agency systems. Required data is easily extractable from appropriate documentation.
Security compliance	System-level information security metrics or an aggregation of information security compliance percentages from, risk assessments, security certification and accreditation, or other sources, organized according to the prioritization criteria categories	Risk Assessments, and security certification and accreditation activities are required for all agencies. Required data can be easily aggregated in the required form.
Corrective action cost	System POA&M	POA&M is a required activity for all agencies. Required data can be easily aggregated in the required form.
Enterprise-Level Information		
Stakeholder rankings of enterprise-wide initiatives	Prioritization sessions with agency information security stakeholders	New activity – requires collaboration among agency information security stakeholders.
Enterprise-wide initiative information security status	Enterprise-level information security metrics or an aggregation of information security compliance percentages from risk assessments, security certification and accreditation, or other sources, organized according to the prioritization criteria categories	Risk assessments and security certification and accreditation activities are required for all agencies. Required data can be easily aggregated in the required form.
Cost of implementing remaining required security controls for enterprise-wide initiatives	Program POA&M	POA&M is a required activity for all agencies. Required data can be easily aggregated in the required form.

Some of the data inputs need to be manipulated further to support the corrective action prioritization process:

---

[39] See Chapter 8, Security Planning, Chapter 10, Risk Management, Chapter 11, Certification, Accreditation, and Security Assessments, and Chapter 14, Configuration Management, of this guide for additional guidance on security roles and responsibilities.

[40] See NIST SP 800-60, *Guide for Mapping Types of Information and Information Systems to Security Categories;* FIPS 199, *Standards for Security Categorization of Federal Information and Information Systems.*

- **Compliance gap:** the difference between the desired and actual compliance with the security requirements. For example, if an information system has completed 80 percent of security certification and accreditation activities, that investment would have a security certification and accreditation compliance gap of 20 percent. (The actual compliance of 80 percent is subtracted from the desired compliance of 100 percent to yield a 20 percent compliance gap.) The smaller the compliance gap, the more compliant the system or enterprise control. For key information security activities, this information is part of the FISMA report.

- **Corrective action impact:** the ratio of compliance gap to corrective action cost. As shown in Figure 5-5, the corrective action impact is calculated by dividing the compliance gap percentage by the cost to implement the corresponding corrective action(s). This ratio provides a proportion of result to cost. The higher the impact proportion, the more "bang for the buck" the

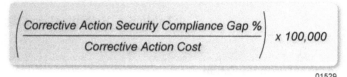

01529

Figure 5-5. Corrective Action Impact Calculation

corrective action will provide. The resulting proportion is multiplied by 100,000 to facilitate further calculations.

After assembling process inputs, conduct the following four steps to complete the prioritization process:

1. Rank-order prioritized corrective action categories according to selected prioritization criteria in order of importance to the agency;
2. Rank-order agency systems according to system category;
3. Calculate the security compliance gaps at the enterprise and investment levels; and
4. Calculate the corrective action impact at the enterprise and investment levels.

Both enterprise- and system-level prioritization should be performed and then overlapped to ensure that appropriate agency priorities receive funding commensurate with their risk levels. Prioritization may be facilitated using a spreadsheet or a more sophisticated automation tool.[41] Visualization of the prioritization may be used to facilitate the decision-making process.

Figure 5-6 demonstrates an example of a corrective action prioritization visualization approach using notional data. From a system-level perspective, Figure 5-6 plots system category along the vertical axis and corrective action impact along the horizontal axis. The notional agency systems are denoted as the small letters at the top of each quadrant. In this example, systems "N" and "F" were found to have category rankings of "high" and corrective action impacts of "great."

---

[41] Figures 4-6 and 4-8 on pages 31 and 34 (respectively) in NIST SP 800-65 provide examples of how spreadsheets can be used to facilitate the prioritization process.

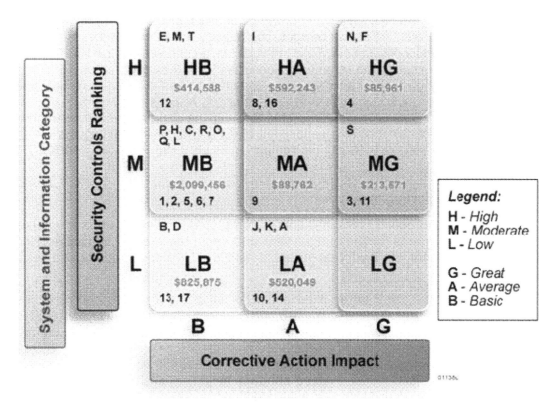

Figure 5-6. Joint Prioritization with Costs

Drawn from the perspective of the enterprise, Figure 5-6 plots agency-determined security controls importance along the vertical axis and corrective action impact along the horizontal axis. The numbers (1-17) represent the seventeen NIST SP 800-53 security control areas used for this example. Security control area 12 ranked "high" in importance but had a "basic" corrective action impact.

The dollar figures in Figure 5-6 represent the total cost to implement all corrective actions within that cell. For example, looking at cell HG, it would cost the agency $85,961 to implement corrective actions for systems "N" and "F" and topic area "4." After plotting all of its systems, the agency should perform executive validation of the placement of the various systems to ensure that stakeholders' priorities are met.

Agency information security stakeholders should review the prioritization results to ensure that the prioritization is appropriate and given the opportunity to reprioritize their inputs if the results of the process are found to be unsatisfactory. Assuming the agency stakeholders agree that all prioritized corrective actions are appropriate, as displayed in Figure 5-6, the analysis can proceed accordingly. As indicated by the axes, the implementation of corrective actions should begin with cell HG and proceed diagonally down to cell LB to ensure that the agency implements the most cost-effective, high-impact corrective actions.

To continue with the example, assume the notional agency has a $2,000,000 budget to implement information security corrective actions. As Figure 5-6 demonstrates, adding the three highest priority cells together (HG, HA, and MG) brings a total of $891,775, which is nearly half of the corrective action budget. The agency would then move to the next tier of prioritization, or cells HB, MA, and LG. Totaling these cells yields a total of $503,350, which combined with the previous total from HG, HA, and MG, yields a running total of $1,395,125. With $604,875 remaining in the corrective action budget, the agency would proceed with prioritization into cells MB and LA. Totaling those two cells yields $2,619,505. Clearly, this total exceeds the remaining corrective action budget, so stakeholders will have to decide on how to allocate the remaining dollars. Should stakeholders determine that the corrective action impact order (G, A, B) is the driving factor, the corrective actions in cell LA will be implemented. If the stakeholders determine that the system and security control category (H, M, L) is the driving factor, the corrective actions from cell MB will be implemented until the remaining $604,875 is expended.[42]

5.7 Develop Supporting Materials

Once prioritizing against requirements is completed, operating units are poised to select their investments for the budget year and begin the process of requesting funding from OMB for the next year to implement the corrective actions and security controls.

The Exhibit 300 is the capture mechanism for all of the analyses and activities required for full internal review (e.g., IRB, CIO). More importantly, Exhibit 300 is the document that OMB uses to assess investments and ultimately make funding decisions, and therefore should be leveraged by agencies to clearly demonstrate the need for life cycle and annual funding requests. The Exhibit 300 is completed for new IT investments and is resubmitted annually for mixed life-cycle and steady-state investments. Operating units should evaluate their prioritized corrective actions and security controls identified during the prioritization process and determine whether the outputs need to be incorporated into an existing investment's Exhibit 300 or whether they will need to create an independent Exhibit 300 for a new investment.

5.8 IRB and Portfolio Management

The IRB reviews and selects investments for the agency portfolio based on the Exhibit 300s forwarded by the operating units. Like the prioritization that occurs at the operating-unit level, the IRB typically uses strategic selection criteria to rank-order the investment pool and usually makes decisions based on agency mission and goals, not just on cost. While security is not the typical driving force behind portfolio management, it is a critical element in the investment strategy because it serves as a qualifier for receiving funding and as a business enabler for those functions which support the agency's mission. After prioritizing and approving select Exhibit 300s, the IRB creates an investment portfolio request for review by OMB.

5.9 Exhibits 53 and 300 and Program Management

Following selection into the agency's IT portfolio, the agency aggregates Exhibit 300s into the Exhibit 53. The Exhibit 53 provides an overview of the agency's entire IT portfolio by listing every IT investment, life cycle, and budget-year cost information.

In addition to containing all investments with Exhibit 300s, the Exhibit 53 also contains other IT investments that do not have Exhibit 300s (e.g., legacy systems with costs below agency thresholds). OMB evaluates an agency's Exhibit 53 and

---

[42] The information presented in this special publication provides an overview of the prioritization process. For a detailed explanation of suggested system- and enterprise-level prioritization procedures, see NIST SP 800-65, pages 28-36.

Exhibit 300s and determines appropriate funding amounts for the budget year based on the justification articulated in the Exhibit 300s. Agencies then receive their budget year funding and must implement or maintain their investments throughout the year by applying allocated funding.

Websites:
Exhibit 300 Information:
http://www.whitehouse.gov/omb/circulars/a11/current_year/s300.pdf

www.csrc.nist.gov

References:
Public Law 107-347 [H.R. 2458], *The E-Government Act of 2002, Title III of this Act is the Federal Information Security Management Act of 2002 (FISMA)*, December 17, 2002.

Office of Management and Budget Circular A-130, *Management of Federal Information Resources*, November 2000.

Federal Information Processing Standard 199, *Requirements for Security Categorization of Federal Information and Information Systems*, February 2004.

Federal Information Processing Standard 200, *Minimum Security Standards for Federal Information and Information Systems*, March 2006.

National Institute of Standards and Technology Special Publication 800-18, *Revision 1, Guide for Developing Security Plans for Federal Information Systems*, February 2006.

National Institute of Standards and Technology Special Publication 800-53A, *Guide for Assessing the Security Controls in Federal Information Systems (draft), April 2006.*

National Institute of Standards and Technology Special Publication 800-37, *Guide for the Security Certification and Accreditation of Federal Information Systems*, May 2004.

National Institute of Standards and Technology Special Publication 800-53, Revision 1, *Recommended Security Controls for Federal Information Systems*, February 2006.

National Institute of Standards and Technology Special Publication 800-55, *Security Metrics Guide for Information Technology Systems*, July 2003.

National Institute of Standards and Technology Special Publication 800-60, *Guide for Mapping Types of Information and Information Systems to Security Categories*, June 2004.

National Institute of Standards and Technology Special Publication 800-65, *Integrating Information Security into the Capital Planning and Investment Control Process,* January 2005.

Office of Management and Budget Circular A-11, *Preparation, Submission, and Execution of the Budget*, 2003.

Chapter 6

6. Interconnecting Systems

A system interconnection is defined as the direct connection of two or more information systems for sharing data and other information resources. Organizations choose to interconnect their information systems for a variety of reasons based on their organizational needs. For example, they may interconnect information systems to exchange data, collaborate on joint projects, or securely store data and backup files.

An interconnection is a direct connection between one organization's system with another system of the same or different organization through a mechanism by which they are joined (the "pipe" through which data is made available, exchanged, or passed one way only). The "pipe" may be a dedicated line that is owned by one of the organizations or is leased from a third party (e.g., Integrated Services Digital Network [ISDN], T1 or T3 line). Alternately, the systems may be connected over a public network (e.g., Internet) using a virtual private network (VPN).

Figure 6-1 depicts the concept of information system interconnection.

01533

Figure 6-1. Information System Interconnection

The following are examples of interconnections:

- System A is connected to System B over a subscriber line leased by System A or System B.
- System A is segmented such that System A1 is integrated with System A but is under different management control: Authorizing Official (AO).
- System B provides data transport services between System A and System C. Here, System B is engaged in two interconnections with Systems A and C.

Levels of system interconnection may vary. For example, some organizations may choose to establish a limited interconnection, whereby users are restricted to a single application or file location with rules governing access. Other organizations may establish a broader interconnection, enabling users to access multiple applications or databases. Still other organizations may establish an interconnection that permits full transparency and access across their respective enterprises.

Interconnecting information systems can expose the participating organizations to risk. If the interconnection is not properly designed, security failures could compromise the connected systems and their data. Similarly, if one of the connected systems is compromised, the interconnection could be used as a conduit to compromise the other system and its data.

Federal policy requires that federal agencies establish interconnection security agreements. Specifically, Office of Management and Budget (OMB) Circular A-130, Appendix III, requires that agencies obtain written management authority before connecting their information systems to other systems, based on a mutually acceptable level of risk. National Institute of Standards and Technology (NIST)

Special Publication (SP) 800-47, *Security Guide for Interconnecting Information Technology Systems*, provides detailed guidance on interconnecting information systems.

6.1 Managing System Interconnections

All federal agencies must explicitly address the subject of interconnecting information systems by establishing formal agreements that specify the technical and security requirements of the interconnection, define the responsibilities of the participating organizations, and specify the rules governing these interconnections. In addition to an A-130, Appendix III, requirement to obtain written management authority before interconnecting information systems, OMB recommends that agencies use NIST SP 800-47 to ensure compliance for connections to non-agency systems.[43]

When organizations are properly managing interconnected systems, the added benefits include greater efficiency, centralized access to data, and greater functionality. The security controls of each of the interconnected systems should be evaluated and meet each other's requirements for implementing security controls that are appropriate for the particular interconnection. Both organizations should specify their requirements regarding the security controls to be implemented in accordance with NIST FIPS 200, *Minimum Security Requirements for Federal Information and Information Systems,* and NIST SP 800-53, *Recommended Security Controls for Federal Information Systems*.

Each system involved in interconnection should be governed by an organization's AO who has the authority to formally assume responsibility for operating a system at an acceptable level of risk. NIST SP 800-53 specifically defines an information systems connections control (specified in Table 6-1) that organizations are required to implement based on an information system's security categorization. Since these categorizations and guidance apply to individual systems, agencies should carefully weigh the associated risks when systems differing in configuration or security controls are interconnected.

Table 6-1. NIST SP 800-53 Information System Connections Control

Identifier	Title	Control
CA-3	Information System Connections	The organization authorizes all connections from the information system to other information systems outside of the accreditation boundary and regularly monitors/controls the system interconnections. Appropriate organizational officials approve information system interconnection agreements.

It is critical that both organizations maintain clear lines of communication to:

- Ensure that the interconnection is properly maintained and that security controls remain effective;
- Facilitate effective change management activities by making it easy for both sides to notify each other about planned system changes that could affect the interconnection; and
- Enable prompt notification by both sides of security incidents and system disruptions and facilitate coordinated response, if necessary.

---

[43] OMB, M-05-15, 'FY05 Reporting Instructions for the Federal Information Security Management Act and Agency Privacy Management.'

Identifying and implementing security controls is vital in protecting the confidentiality, integrity, and availability of the connected systems and the data that is transferred between the systems. If security controls are not in place or if they are configured improperly, the process of establishing the interconnection could expose the information systems to unauthorized access. Agencies should select applicable controls from NIST SP 800-53, based on the security categorization of the systems involved in the interconnection from FIPS 199, *Standards for Security Categorization of Federal Information and Information Systems,* and NIST SP 800-60, *Guide for Mapping Types of Information and Information Systems to Security Categories*. The security controls should be appropriately selected in consideration of the systems that will be connected and the environment in which the interconnection will operate.

One or both organizations should review the security controls for the interconnection at least annually or whenever a significant change occurs to either system or the operational environment. This review is intended to ensure that all controls are operating properly and still provide the requisite degree of system and data security.[44]

6.2 Life-Cycle Management Approach

NIST SP 800-47 details a four-phase "life-cycle management" approach for interconnecting information systems that emphasizes proper attention to information security:

- Phase 1: Planning the Interconnection;
- Phase 2: Establishing the Interconnection;
- Phase 3: Maintaining the Interconnection; and
- Phase 4: Disconnecting the Interconnection.

6.2.1 Phase 1: Planning the Interconnection

The process of connecting two or more information systems begins with a planning phase, where the participating organizations perform preliminary activities and examine all relevant technical, security, and administrative issues. The planning phase ensures that the interconnection will operate as efficiently and securely as possible. Six steps are recommended for planning a system interconnection. Figure 6-2 illustrates the step-by-step process to plan a system interconnection. A more detailed process is described in the following paragraphs.

---

[44] See NIST SP 800-30, *Risk Management Guide for Information Technology Systems*; Chapter 10, Risk Management, and Chapter 11, Certification, Accreditation, and Security Assessments, of this guide can be consulted for additional guidance on security control reviews.

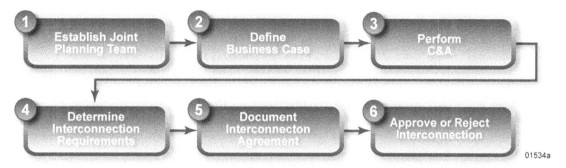

Figure 6-2. Steps to Plan a System Interconnection

Step 1: Establish a Joint Planning Team

The organizations should consider establishing a joint planning team composed of appropriate management and technical staff that includes program managers, system security officers, system administrators, network administrators, and system architects. The typical joint planning team is responsible for coordinating all aspects of the planning process and ensuring that it has both clear direction and sufficient resources. It also must have the commitment and support of the system and data owners, and other senior managers.

Step 2: Define the Business Case

Both organizations should work together to define the purpose of the interconnection, determine how it will support their mission requirements, and identify potential costs and risks. Defining the business case will establish the basis of the interconnection and facilitate the planning process. Factors that should be considered are estimated costs (e.g., staffing, equipment, facilities), expected benefits (e.g., improved efficiency), and potential risks (e.g., technical, legal, and financial).

Step 3: Perform Certification and Accreditation

Establishing an interconnection may represent a significant change to the connected systems. Before proceeding further, each organization should consider recertification and reaccreditation of its respective system(s) to verify that security protections remain acceptable. A full security certification and accreditation might not be necessary, however, if the system continues to operate within an acceptable level of risk; in that case, an abbreviated certification and accreditation would suffice.[45]

Step 4: Determine Interconnection Requirements

The joint planning team should identify and examine all relevant technical, security, and administrative requirements surrounding the proposed interconnection.

Step 5: Document Interconnection Agreement

The interconnection security agreement (ISA) is a security document that specifies the technical and security requirements for establishing, operating, and maintaining the interconnection. It also supports the memorandum of

---

[45] See NIST SP 800-37, *Guide for the Security Certification and Accreditation of Federal Information Systems*, and Chapter 11, Certification, Accreditation, and Security Assessments, of this guide can be consulted for additional guidance on C&A.

understanding/memorandum of agreement (MOU/MOA) between the organizations. Specifically, the ISA documents the requirements for connecting the information systems, describes the security controls that will be used to protect the systems and data, contains a topological drawing of the interconnection, and provides a signature line.

The joint planning team should document an agreement governing the interconnection and the terms under which the organizations will abide. The agreement should be based on the team's review of all relevant technical, security, and administrative requirements identified and examined in Step 4.

The MOU/MOA documents the terms and conditions for sharing data and information resources. It defines the purpose of the interconnection, identifies relevant authorities, specifies the responsibilities of each organization, defines the apportionment of costs, and identifies the timeline for terminating or reauthorizing the interconnection. In order to operate as an instrument that can be enforced by any agency that is a party to the interconnection, the MOU/MOA must be signed by an organization official, typically the authorizing official (AO). Lastly, because the ISA and the MOU/MOA may contain sensitive information, the original document and any copies should be protected appropriately against unauthorized disclosure or modification, damage, or destruction.

Step 6: Approve or Reject System Interconnection

The joint planning team should submit the ISA and the MOU/MOA to the AO of each organization, requesting approval for the interconnection. Upon receipt, the AOs should review the ISA, the MOU/MOA, and any other relevant documentation or activities. Organizations may combine ISAs and MOU/MOAs to simplify their management processes and reduce paperwork if these two documents fall within the purview of the same AO. When combining ISAs and MOU/MOAs, organizations must ensure that the contents and the intent of these two documents remain unaltered.

Based on this review, the AOs should decide on one of the following:

- Approve the interconnection;
- Grant interim approval; or
- Reject the interconnection.

6.2.2 Phase 2: Establishing the Interconnection

After the system interconnection is planned and approved, it can be implemented. The recommended steps for establishing the system interconnection are provided in Figure 6-3.

Figure 6-3. Recommended Steps for Establishing the Interconnection

Step 1: Develop an Implementation Plan

To ensure that the information systems are connected properly and securely, the joint planning team should develop a system interconnection implementation plan. At a minimum, the implementation plan should:

- Describe the information systems that will be connected;
- Identify the sensitivity or classification level of data that will be made available, exchanged, or passed one way across the interconnection;
- Identify personnel who will establish and maintain the interconnection and specify their responsibilities;
- Identify implementation tasks and procedures;
- Identify and describe security controls that will be used to protect the confidentiality, integrity, and availability of the connected systems and data;
- Provide test procedures and measurement criteria to ensure that the interconnection operates properly and securely;
- Specify training requirements for users, including a training schedule; and
- Cite or include all relevant documentation, such as system security plans, design specifications, and standard operating procedures (SOPs).

Step 2: Execute the Implementation Plan

After the implementation plan is developed, it should be reviewed and approved by senior members of the planning team and then executed. A list of recommended tasks for establishing an interconnection includes:

- Implement or configure security controls;
- Install or configure hardware and software;
- Integrate applications;
- Conduct operational and security assessments;
- Conduct security training and awareness;
- Update system security plans; and
- Perform recertification and reaccreditation.

Procedures associated with each task should be described in the implementation plan.

Step 3: Activate the Interconnection

Both parties should activate the interconnection following the implementation plan execution. Each agency should closely and frequently examine the system's audit logs and the types of assistance requested by the system's users during this time to ensure that it operates properly and securely. Lastly, the appropriate agency should promptly document and address any security weaknesses or problems.

6.2.3 Phase 3: Maintaining the Interconnection

After the interconnection is established, the participating organizations must actively maintain it to ensure that it operates properly and securely. The following activities are recommended for maintaining the interconnection:

- Maintain the equipment;
- Manage user profiles;
- Conduct security reviews;
- Analyze audit logs;
- Report and respond to security incidents;
- Coordinate contingency planning activities;
- Perform change management; and
- Maintain system security plans.

6.2.4 Phase 4: Disconnecting the Interconnection

Phase-out may either be planned or it may be an emergency. Organizations may wish to restore some of the disconnections but not others.

6.3 Terminating Interconnection

An organization might have a variety of reasons to terminate an interconnection, for instance, changed business needs, cost considerations, or changes in system configuration. The decision to terminate the interconnection should be made by the system owner with the advice of appropriate management and technical staff. Before terminating the interconnection, the initiating party should provide written notice to the receiving party. In turn, the receiving party should acknowledge receipt of the notification. The notification should describe the reason(s) for the disconnection, provide the proposed timeline for the disconnection, and identify technical and management staff that will conduct the disconnection.

The schedule for terminating the interconnection should permit a reasonable time period for internal business planning so both sides can make appropriate arrangements. In addition, staff from both organizations should coordinate to determine the logistics of the disconnection and the disposition of shared data, including purging and overwriting sensitive data. The disconnection should be conducted when the impact on users is minimal. Following the disconnection, each organization should update its system security plan and related documents.

6.3.1 Emergency Disconnection

If one or both organizations detect an attack, intrusion attempt, or other contingency that exploits or jeopardizes the connected systems or their data, it might be necessary to abruptly terminate the interconnection without providing written notice to the other party. This extraordinary measure should be taken only in extreme circumstances and only after consultation with appropriate technical staff and senior management.

The decision to make the emergency disconnection should be made by the system owner (or a designated staff member) and implemented by technical staff. The system owner or designee should immediately notify the other party verbally and receive confirmation of the notification. Both parties should work together to isolate and investigate the incident, in accordance with incident response procedures. If necessary, law enforcement authorities should be notified, and evidence should be preserved.

The initiating party should provide a *written* notification to the other party in a timely manner (e.g., within five days). The notification should describe the nature of the incident, explain why and how the interconnection was terminated, and identify actions taken to isolate and investigate the incident. The notification should also specify when and under what conditions the interconnection may be restored, if appropriate.

6.3.2 Restoration of Interconnection

Both organizations may choose to restore the system interconnection after it has been terminated. The decision to restore the interconnection should be based on the cause and duration of the disconnection. For example, if the interconnection was terminated because of an attack, intrusion, or other contingency, both parties should implement appropriate countermeasures to prevent a recurrence of the problem. If necessary, they also should modify the ISA and MOU/MOA to address issues requiring attention. Alternately, if the interconnection has been terminated for more than 90 days, each party should perform a risk assessment on its respective system and reexamine all relevant planning and implementation requirements, including developing a new ISA and MOU/MOA.

Sample MOU/MOA and ISA Checklist follow.

Annex 6.A Sample MOU/MOA

This annex provides a sample MOU/MOA template that agencies can use as a starting point for developing their own MOU/MOAs. This sample does not cover all possible scenarios and should be used as an example only.

FOR OFFICIAL USE ONLY

(MEMORANDUM OF UNDERSTANDING / MEMORANDUM OF AGREEMENT)

SUPERSEDES: (None or document title and date)

INTRODUCTION The purpose of this memorandum is to establish a management agreement between "Organization A" and "Organization B" regarding the development, management, operation, and security of a connection between "System A," owned by Organization A, and "System B," owned by Organization B. This agreement will govern the relationship between Organization A and Organization B, including designated managerial and technical staff, in the absence of a common management authority.

AUTHORITY The authority for this agreement is based on "Proclamation A" issued by the Agency Head on (date).

BACKGROUND It is the intent of both parties to this agreement to interconnect the following information technology (IT) systems to exchange data between "ABC database" and "XYZ database." Organization A requires the use of Organization B's ABC database, and Organization B requires the use of Organization A's XYZ database, as approved and directed by the Agency Head in Proclamation A. The expected benefit of the interconnection is to expedite the processing of data associated with "Project R" within prescribed timelines. Each information system is described below:

SYSTEM A
– Name
– Function
– Location
– Description of data, including sensitivity or classification level and security categorization/impact level

SYSTEM B
– Name
– Function
– Location
– Description of data, including sensitivity or classification level and security categorization/impact level

COMMUNICATIONS

Frequent formal communications are essential to ensure the successful management and operation of the interconnection. The parties agree to maintain open lines of communication between designated staff at both the managerial and technical levels. All communications described herein must be conducted in writing unless otherwise noted. The owners of System A and System B agree to designate and provide contact information for technical leads for their respective system, and to facilitate direct contacts between technical leads to support the management and operation of the interconnection. To safeguard the confidentiality, integrity, and availability of the connected systems and the data they store, process, and transmit, the parties agree to provide notice of specific events within the time frames indicated below:

Security Incidents: Technical staff will *immediately* notify their designated counterparts by telephone or e-mail when a security incident(s) is detected, so the other party may take steps to determine whether its system has been compromised and to take appropriate security precautions. The system owner will receive *formal notification* in writing within five (5) business days after detection of the incident(s).

Disasters and Other Contingencies: Technical staff will immediately notify their designated counterparts by telephone or e-mail in the event of a disaster or other contingency that disrupts the normal operation of one or both of the connected systems.

Material Changes to System Configuration: Planned technical changes to the system architecture will be reported to technical staff before such changes are implemented. The initiating party agrees to conduct a risk assessment based on the new system architecture and to modify and re-sign the ISA within one (1) month of implementation.

New Interconnections: The initiating party will notify the other party at least one (1) month *before* it connects its information system with any other information system, including systems that are owned and operated by third parties.

Personnel Changes: The parties agree to provide notification of the separation or long-term absence of their respective system owner or technical lead. In addition, both parties will provide notification of any changes in point of contact information. Both parties also will provide notification of changes to user profiles, including users who resign or change job responsibilities.

INTERCONNECTION SECURITY AGREEMENT

The technical details of the interconnection will be documented in an Interconnection Security Agreement (ISA). The parties agree to work together to develop the ISA, which must be signed by both parties before the interconnection is activated. Proposed changes to either system or the interconnecting medium will be reviewed and evaluated to determine the potential impact on the interconnection. The ISA will be renegotiated before changes are implemented. Signatories to the ISA shall be the AO for each system.

SECURITY

Both parties agree to work together to ensure the joint security of the connected systems and the data they store, process, and transmit, as specified in the ISA. Based on National Institute of Standards and Technology Special Publication 800-53, *Recommended Security Controls for Federal Information Systems*, both parties should authorize all connections from the information system to other information systems outside of that accreditation boundary and monitor and control the system interconnections on an ongoing basis. Each party should identify security controls that apply to the interconnection based on each system's information security categorization and impact level and agree on a mutual set of applicable controls. Each party certifies that its respective system is designed, managed, and operated in compliance with all relevant federal laws, regulations, and policies, and will ensure that appropriate security controls are maintained throughout the life of this MOU/MOA.

PRIVACY REQUIREMENTS

Both parties agree to examine privacy issues related to data that will be exchanged or passed over the interconnection and determine whether such use is restricted under current statutes, regulations, or policies. Examples of data that might be restricted include personally identifiable information such as names and social security numbers, or confidential business information such as contractor bid rates and trade secrets. Each party should consult with its Privacy Officer or Legal Counsel to determine whether such information may be shared or transferred. Permission to exchange or transfer data should be documented, along with a commitment to protect such data.

COST CONSIDERATIONS

Both parties agree to equally share the costs of the interconnecting mechanism and/or media, but no such expenditures or financial commitments shall be made without the written concurrence of both parties. Modifications to either system that are necessary to support the interconnection are the responsibility of the respective system owners' organization.

TIMELINE

This agreement will remain in effect for one (1) year after the last date on either signature in the signature block below. After one (1) year, this agreement will expire without further action. If the parties wish to extend this agreement, they may do so by reviewing, updating, and reauthorizing this agreement. The newly signed agreement should explicitly supersede this agreement, which should be referenced by title and date. If one or both of the parties wish to terminate this agreement prematurely, they may do so upon 30 days' advanced notice or in the event of a security incident that necessitates an immediate response.

SIGNATORY AUTHORITY

I agree to the terms of this Memorandum of Understanding / Memorandum of Agreement.

(Organization A Official)   **(Organization B Official)**

_____   _____
(Signature   Date)   (Signature   Date)

Annex 6.B ISA Checklist

This annex provides a generic checklist that agencies may use in developing their ISAs to ensure that they have discussed requirements covered in this section.

	ISA CHECKLIST	YES	NO
1	**ISA Requirements:**		
A	Is there a formal requirement and justification for connecting two systems?		
B	Are there two systems being interconnected? 　　If YES, have the systems been specified? 　　If NO, the two systems need to be specified.		
C	Is there a list of benefits of required interconnection(s)?		
D	Is the agency name or organization that initiated the requirement listed?		
2	**System Security Considerations:**		
A	Has a security certification and accreditation of the system been completed?		
B	Has the security certification and accreditation status been verified?		
C	Are there security features in place to protect the confidentiality, integrity, and availability of the data and the systems being interconnected?		
D	Has each system's security categorization been identified per FIPS 199?		
E	Have minimum controls been identified for each system in accordance with NIST SP 800-53?		
F	Have both parties answered each subject item regardless if the subjected item only affects one party? If No, both parties must go back and answer each item.		
G	Is there a general description of the information/data being made available, exchanged, or passed?		
H	Is there a description of the information services (e.g., e-mail, file transfer protocol, database query, file query, general computational services) offered over the interconnected system by each participating organization?		
I	Have system users been identified and has an approval been put in place?		
J	Is there a description of all system security technical services pertinent to the secure exchange of information/data among and between the systems in question?		
K	Are there documented rules of behavior for users of each system in the interconnection?		
L	Are there titles of the formal security policy(ies) that govern each system?		
M	Are there procedures for incidents related to the interconnection?		
N	Are there audit requirements?		
3	**Topological Drawing:**		
A	Is there a descriptive technical specification for the connections?		
4	**Signatory Authority:** ISA is valid for one year after the last date on either signature below. At that time, it will be reviewed, updated if necessary, and revalidated. This agreement may be terminated upon 30 days advanced notice by either party or in the event of a security exception that would necessitate an immediate response.		

Website:
www.csrc.nist.gov

References:
Federal Information Processing Standard 199, *Standards for Security Categorization of Federal Information and Information Systems*, February 2004.

Federal Information Processing Standard 200, *Minimum Security Requirements for Federal Information and Information Systems,* March 2006.

National Institute of Standards and Technology, Information Technology Laboratory (ITL) Bulletin: *Secure Interconnections for Information Technology Systems,* February 2003.

National Institute of Standards and Technology Special Publication 800-30, *Risk Management Guide for Information Technology Systems*, July 2002.

National Institute of Standards and Technology Special Publication 800-37, *Guide for the Security Certification and Accreditation of Federal Information Systems*, May 2004.

National Institute of Standards and Technology Special Publication 800-42, *Guidelines on Network Security Testing*, October 2003.

National Institute of Standards and Technology Special Publication 800-47, *Security Guide for Interconnecting Information Technology Systems*, August 2002.

National Institute of Standards and Technology Special Publication 800-53, Revision 1, *Recommended Security Controls for Federal Information System,* February 2006.

National Institute of Standards and Technology Special Publication 800-60, *Guide for Mapping Types of Information and Information Systems to Security Categories*, June 2004.

Chapter 7

7. Performance Measures

A performance measures program provides numerous organizational and financial benefits to federal agencies. Agencies can develop information security metrics that measure the effectiveness of their security program, and provide data to be analyzed and used by program managers and system owners to isolate problems, justify investment requests, and target funds specifically to the areas in need of improvement. By using metrics to target security investments, agencies can get the best value from available resources. The typical information performance management program consists of four interdependent components: senior management support, security policies and procedures, quantifiable performance metrics, and analyses.

Strong senior management support establishes a focus on security within the highest levels of the organization. Without a solid foundation (e.g., proactive support of those persons in positions that control information resources), the effectiveness of the security metrics program can fail when pressured by politics and budget limitations. The second component of an effective security metrics program is practical security policies and procedures backed by the authority necessary to enforce compliance. Metrics are not easily obtainable in the absence of policies and procedures. The third component is developing and establishing quantifiable performance metrics that are designed to capture and provide meaningful performance data. To provide meaningful data, quantifiable security metrics must be based on information security performance goals and objectives, and be easily obtainable, repeatable, relevant, useful, and measurable. Finally, the security metrics program itself must emphasize consistent, periodic analysis of the metrics data. The results of this analysis are used to apply lessons learned, improve the effectiveness of existing security controls, and plan future controls to meet new security requirements as they occur. Accurate data collection must be a priority with stakeholders and users if the collected data is to be meaningful to the management and improvement of the overall security program.

A number of existing laws, rules, and regulations cite information technology (IT) performance measurement in general and information security performance measurement in particular, as requirements. These laws include the Clinger-Cohen Act, Government Performance and Results Act (GPRA), Government Paperwork Elimination Act (GPEA), and the Federal Information Security Management Act (FISMA).

National Institute of Standards and Technology (NIST) Special Publication (SP) 800-55, *Security Metrics Guide for Information Technology Systems*, provides guidance on how an organization, by using metrics, identifies the adequacy of in-place security controls, policies, and procedures. It provides an approach to help management decide where to invest in additional security protection resources or how to identify and evaluate nonproductive controls. It explains the metrics development and implementation process and how it can also be used to adequately justify security control investments. The results of an effective metrics program can provide useful data for directing the allocation of information security resources and should simplify the preparation of performance-related reports.

Fiscal constraints and market conditions compel government and industry to operate on reduced budgets. In such an environment, it is difficult to justify broad investments in the information security infrastructure. Historically, arguments for investing in specific areas of information security lack detail and specificity and fail to adequately mitigate specific system risk. Information security metrics can facilitate the capital planning and investment control (CPIC) process by providing quantifiable information for business case development.[46] Information security metrics can also assist with determining the effectiveness of implemented information security processes, procedures, and controls by relating results of information security activities (e.g., incident data, revenue lost to cyber attacks) to the respective requirements and to information security investments.

Departments and agencies can also demonstrate compliance with applicable laws, such as FISMA, rules, and regulations by implementing and maintaining an information security metrics program as described in this handbook. Information security metrics will assist in satisfying the annual FISMA reporting requirement by providing an infrastructure for organized data collection, analysis, and reporting. Information security metrics can also be used as input into the Government Accountability Office (GAO) and Inspector General (IG) audits.

7.1 Metric Types

Metrics are tools that support decision making. Like experience, external mandates, and strategies, metrics are one element of a manager's toolkit for making and substantiating decisions. Metrics are used to answer three basic questions:

- *"Am I implementing the tasks for which I am responsible?"* Consider the example of a program manager with responsibility for 250 information systems. Among other things, that manager is responsible for the security certification and accreditation of those systems. A commonly used implementation metric for security certification and accreditation is the percentage of systems accredited.

- *"How efficiently or effectively am I accomplishing those tasks?"* Such metrics often answer more complex questions after an activity is fully implemented. For example, federal law requires that security certification and accreditation take place following a major system change. One might measure the efficiency of a security certification and accreditation program by determining the time lag between each major system change and that system's renewed accreditation. Or one might measure the effectiveness of a security certification and accreditation program by determining the number of accredited systems whose certification process included the creation of a system security plan.

- *"What impact are those tasks having on the mission?"* Activities are initially selected with the belief that they will contribute to the mission. After an activity is shown to be fully implemented, managers must validate that the activity is delivering the expected benefit. These metrics are the most difficult to generate. A security certification and accreditation process may prove to have an impact by showing that fewer interruptions or losses of data due to security incidents are experienced among correctly accredited systems than among incorrectly accredited or nonaccredited systems.

---

[46] See NIST SP 800-65, *Integrating Security into the Capital Planning and Investment Control Process*, and Chapter 5, Capital Planning, of this guide for additional guidance on business case development.

7.2 Metrics Development and Implementation Approach

Two processes guide the establishment and operation of an information security metrics program: metrics development and metrics implementation. The metrics development process establishes the initial set of metrics and selection of the metrics subset appropriate for an organization at a given time. The metrics program implementation process operates a metrics program that is iterative by nature and ensures that appropriate aspects of information security are measured for a specific time period.

7.3 Metrics Development Process

Figure 7-1 illustrates the place of information security metrics within a larger organizational context and demonstrates that information security metrics can be used to progressively measure implementation, efficiency, effectiveness, and the business impact of information security activities within organizations or for specific systems.

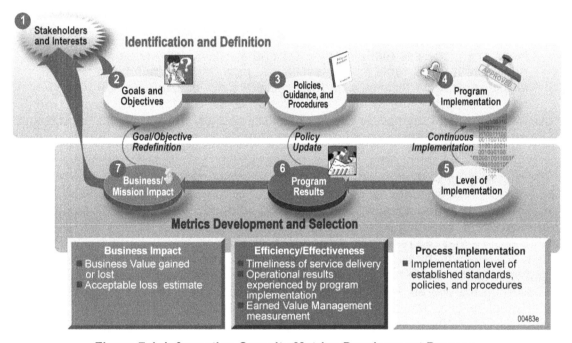

Figure 7-1. Information Security Metrics Development Process

The information security metrics development process consists of two major activities:

1. Identifying and defining the current information security program; and

2. Developing and selecting specific metrics to measure implementation, efficiency, effectiveness, and the impact of the security controls.

The process steps do not need to be sequential. Rather, the process illustrated in Figure 7-1 provides a framework for thinking about metrics and aids in identifying metrics to be developed for each system. The type of metric depends on where the system is within its life cycle and on the maturity of the information system security program. This framework facilitates tailoring metrics to a specific organization and to the different stakeholder groups present within each organization.

Phases 5, 6, and 7, depicted in Figure 7-1, involve developing metrics that measure process implementation, effectiveness and efficiency, and mission impact. The specific aspect of information security that metrics will focus on at any given point will depend on information security program maturity. Implementation evidence, required to prove higher levels of effectiveness, will change from establishing existence of policy and procedures to quantifying implementation of these policies and procedures, then to quantifying results of implementation of policies and procedures, and ultimately to identifying the impact of implementation on the organization's mission.

Based on existing policies and procedures, the universe of possible metrics can be prohibitively large; therefore, agencies should prioritize metrics to ensure that the final set selected for initial implementation has the following attributes:

- Facilitates improvement of high-priority security control implementation. High priority may be defined by the latest GAO or IG reports, results of a risk assessment, or an internal organizational goal;

- Uses data that can realistically be obtained from existing processes and data repositories; and

- Measures processes that already exist and are relatively stable. Measuring nonexistent or unstable processes will not provide meaningful information about security performance and will therefore not be useful for targeting specific aspects of performance. On the other hand, attempting such measurement may not be entirely useless, because such a metric will certainly produce poor results and will therefore identify an area that needs improvement.

Metrics can be derived from existing data sources, including security certification and accreditation, security assessments, plan of action and milestones (POA&M), incident statistics, and agency-initiated or independent reviews.[47] Agencies may decide to use a weighting scale to differentiate the importance of selected metrics and to ensure that the results accurately reflect existing security program priorities. This process would involve assigning values to each metric based on the importance of a metric in the context of the overall security program. Metrics weighting should be based on the overall risk mitigation goals, is likely to reflect higher criticality of department-level initiatives versus smaller-scale initiatives, and is a useful tool that facilitates integration of information security into the departmental capital planning process.

A phased approach may be required to identify short-, mid-, and long-term metrics in which the implementation time frame depends on a combination of system-level effectiveness, metric priority, data availability, and process stability. Once applicable metrics that contain the qualities described above are identified, they will need to be documented with supporting detail, including frequency of data collection, data source, formula for calculation, implementation evidence for measured activity, and a guide for metric data interpretation. Other information about each metric can be defined based on an organization's processing and business requirements.

---

[47] See NIST SP 800-30, *Risk Management Guide for Information Technology Systems*, Chapter 10, Risk Management, and Chapter 11, Certification, Accreditation, and Security Assessments, of this guide for additional guidance on security assessments.

7.4 Metrics Program Implementation

Information security metrics should be used for monitoring information security control performance and initiating performance improvement actions. This iterative process consists of six phases, depicted in Figure 7-2.

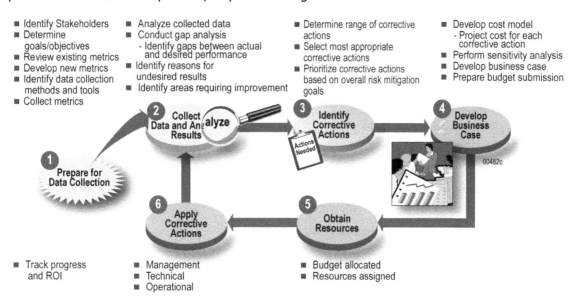

- Identify Stakeholders
- Determine goals/objectives
- Review existing metrics
- Develop new metrics
- Identify data collection methods and tools
- Collect metrics

- Analyze collected data
- Conduct gap analysis
  - Identify gaps between actual and desired performance
- Identify reasons for undesired results
- Identify areas requiring improvement

- Determine range of corrective actions
- Select most appropriate corrective actions
- Prioritize corrective actions based on overall risk mitigation goals

- Develop cost model
  - Project cost for each corrective action
- Perform sensitivity analysis
- Develop business case
- Prepare budget submission

- Track progress and ROI

- Management
- Technical
- Operational

- Budget allocated
- Resources assigned

Figure 7-2. Information Security Metrics Program Implementation Process

7.4.1 Prepare for Data Collection

Phase 1 of the process, Prepare for Data Collection, involves activities that are key for establishing a comprehensive information security metrics program. These activities include the information security metrics identification, definition, development, and selection activities, and developing a metrics program implementation plan.

After the metrics have been identified, specific implementation steps should be defined on how to collect, analyze, and report the metrics. These steps should be documented in the metrics program implementation plan. The following items may be included in the plan:

- Metrics roles and responsibilities, including responsibilities for data collection (both soliciting and submitting), analysis, and reporting;

- An audience for the plan;

- Process of metrics collection, analysis, and reporting that is tailored to the specific organizational structure, processes, policies, and procedures;

- Details of coordination with the chief information officer (CIO), such as with risk assessment, security certification and accreditation, and FISMA reporting activities;

- Details of coordination between the CIO and other functions within the agency, external to the CIO (e.g., Information Assurance (IA), if separate from the CIO; physical security; personnel security; and critical infrastructure protection [CIP]) to ensure that the metrics data collection is streamlined and nonintrusive;

- Creation or selection of data collection and tracking tools;

- Modifications of data collection and tracking tools; and
- Metrics summary reporting formats.

7.4.2 Collect Data and Analyze Results

Phase 2 of the process, Collect Data and Analyze Results, involves activities that are essential for ensuring that the collected metrics are used to gain an understanding of system security and to identify appropriate improvement actions. This phase includes the following activities:

- Collect metrics data according to the processes defined in the metrics program implementation plan;
- Consolidate collected data and store in a format (i.e., a database or a spreadsheet) conducive to data analysis and reporting;
- Conduct gap analysis, compare collected measurements with targets if defined, and identify gaps between actual and desired performance;
- Identify causes of poor performance; and
- Identify areas requiring improvement.

The causes of poor performance can often be identified using the data from more than one metric. For example, determining that the percentage of approved security plans is unacceptably low would not be helpful for determining how to correct the problem. To determine the cause of low compliance, collect information on the reasons for low percentages (e.g., lack of guidance, insufficient expertise, or conflicting priorities). This information can be collected as separate metrics or as implementation evidence for the percentage of approved security plans. Once this information is collected and compiled, the agency should develop a correction plan to address the root cause of the problem.

Root causes for faulty security run the gamut between highly technical misconfiguration issues to lack of training or outdated policies or practices. Below are examples of causation factors that contribute to poor security control implementation and effectiveness:

- Resources—insufficient human, monetary, or other resources;
- Training—lack of appropriate training for the personnel installing, administering, maintaining, or using the systems;
- System Upgrades—security patches that have been removed but not replaced during the operating system upgrades;
- Configuration Management (CM) Practices—new or upgraded systems that are not configured with required security settings and patches;
- Software Compatibility—security patches or upgrades that are incompatible with software applications supported by the system;
- Awareness and Commitment—lack of management awareness and/or commitment to security;
- Policies and Procedures—lack of policies and procedures that are required to ensure existence, use, and audit of required security functions;
- Architectures—poor system and security architectures that make systems vulnerable; and

- Inefficient Processes—inefficient planning and communication processes that influence the metrics.

7.4.3   Identify Corrective Actions

Phase 3 of the process, Identify Corrective Actions, involves developing a plan that will provide the roadmap of how to close the implementation gap identified in Phase 2. This phase includes the following activities:

- **Determine Range of Corrective Actions**. Based on the results and causation factors, identify corrective actions that could be applied to each performance issue. Corrective actions may include changing system configurations; training security staff, system administrator staff, or regular users; purchasing security tools; changing system architecture; establishing new processes and procedures; and updating security policies.

- **Prioritize Corrective Actions Based on Overall Risk Mitigation Goals**. Several corrective actions may be applicable to a single performance issue; however, some may be inappropriate if they are inconsistent with the magnitude of the problem or are too costly. Applicable corrective actions should be prioritized for each performance issue in the ascending order of cost and descending order of impact. The risk management process, described in NIST SP 800-30, *Risk Management Guide for Information Technology Systems*, should be used for prioritizing corrective actions.[48] If weights were assigned to metrics in Phase 1, *Prepare for Data Collection*, they should be used to prioritize corrective actions. Alternatively, weights may be assigned to corrective actions in Phase 3, *Identify Corrective Actions,* based on the criticality of implementing specific corrective actions, the cost of corrective actions, and the magnitude of corrective actions' impact on the organization's security posture.

- **Select Most Appropriate Corrective Actions**. Up to three corrective actions from the top of the list of prioritized corrective actions should be selected for conducting a full cost-benefit analysis. These selections should then be appropriately reflected in the agency or system POA&Ms.

7.4.4   Develop Business Case and Obtain Resources

Phases 4 and 5, Develop Business Case and Obtain Resources, respectively, address the budgeting cycle required for obtaining resources needed for implementing the remediation actions identified in Phase 3. The steps to develop a business case are based on industry practices and mandated guidance, including Office of Management and Budget (OMB) Circular A-11, the Clinger-Cohen Act, and GPRA. The results of the prior three phases will be included in the business case as supporting evidence. NIST SP 800-55 provides guidance on security practitioners' inputs into the CPIC process and on their role in core development.

Each agency should follow agency-specific business case guidance during this phase. Typically, the components and analysis of the business facilitate the completion of internal and external budget requests. A thorough examination of the business case will support and facilitate the obtaining resources process.

---

[48] Also see Chapter 10, Risk Management, and Chapter 11, Certification, Accreditation, and Security Assessments, of this guide for additional guidance on prioritizing corrective actions.

7.4.5 Apply Corrective Actions

Phase 6 of the process, Apply Corrective Actions, involves implementing corrective actions as determined through data analysis and as defined in an applicable business case or a POA&M. After corrective actions are applied, the cycle completes itself and restarts with subsequent data collection and analysis. Iterative data collection, analysis, and reporting will track the progress of corrective actions through the POA&M, among others, measure improvement, and identify areas for further improvement to be included in tactical plans, Program Management Plans, or other agency planning mechanisms. The iterative nature of the cycle ensures that the progress is monitored, and the corrective actions are affecting system security control implementation in an intended way. Frequent performance measurements will ensure that if corrective actions are not implemented as planned, or if their actual effect is not the desired effect, quick course corrections can be made internally by the agency, thus avoiding the unveiling of problems during external audits, security certification and accreditation efforts, or other similar activities.

Website:
www.csrc.nist.gov

References:
Public Law 107-347 [H.R. 2458], *The E-Government Act of 2002, Title III of this Act is the Federal Information Security Management Act of 2002 (FISMA)*, December 17, 2002.

Office of Management and Budget Circular A-130, *Management of Federal Information Resources*, November 2000.

National Institute of Standards and Technology Special Publication 800-30, *Risk Management Guide for Information Technology Systems*, July 2002.

National Institute of Standards and Technology Special Publication 800-55, *Security Metrics Guide for Information Technology Systems*, July 2003.

Chapter 8

8. Security Planning

Today's rapidly changing technical environment requires that federal agencies adopt a minimum set of security controls to protect their information and information systems. The purpose of the system security plan is to provide an overview of the security requirements of the system and describe the controls in place or planned for meeting those requirements. The system security plan also delineates responsibilities and expected behavior of all individuals who access the system. It should reflect input from various managers with responsibilities concerning the system, including information owners, the system owner, and the senior agency information security officer (SAISO). Agencies, at their discretion, can include additional information in the basic plan and add sections to the basic format prescribed herein, as long as the major sections described in this document are adequately covered and readily identifiable.

Program managers, system owners, and security personnel in the organization must understand the system security planning process. In addition, users of the information system and those responsible for defining system requirements should also be familiar with the system security planning process, as the system security plan is an important deliverable in the system development life cycle (SDLC) process.[49] Those responsible for implementing and managing information systems must participate in addressing security controls to be applied to their systems.

Federal Information Processing Standard (FIPS) 200, *Minimum Security Requirements for Federal Information and Information Systems*, specifies the minimum security requirements for federal information and information systems in seventeen security-related areas. Federal agencies must meet the minimum security requirements defined in FIPS 200 by using the security controls in National Institute of Standards and Technology (NIST) Special Publication (SP) 800-53, *Recommended Security Controls for Federal Information Systems*, and NIST SP 800-18 Rev.1, *Guide for Developing Security Plans for Federal Information Systems*, which provides a Systems Security Plan Template in Appendix A of the document. The guidance below provides basic information on how to prepare a system security plan in accordance with applicable federal requirements, and it is easily adaptable to a variety of organizational structures.

8.1 Major Applications, General Support Systems, and Minor Applications

All information systems must be covered by a system security plan and labeled as a major application (MA)[50] or general support system (GSS).[51] Specific system

---

[49] See NIST Publication 800-64, Security Considerations in the Information System Development Life Cycle, and Chapter 3, System Development Life Cycle, of this guide for additional guidance on the SDLC.

[50] Office of Management and Budget (OMB) Circular A-130, Appendix III, defines major application as an application that requires special attention to security due to the risk and magnitude of harm resulting from the loss, misuse, or unauthorized access to or modification of the information in the application.

[51] OMB Circular A-130, Appendix III, defines general support system as an interconnected set of information resources under the same direct management control that shares common functionality. It normally includes hardware, software, information, data, applications, communications, and people.

security plans for minor applications[52] are not required because the security controls for those applications are typically provided by the GSS or MA in which they operate. In those cases where the minor application is not connected to an MA or GSS, the minor application should be briefly described in a GSS plan that either has a common physical location or is supported by the same organization.

8.2 Security Planning Roles and Responsibilities

Agencies should develop policy on the system security planning process. System security plans are living documents that require periodic review, modification, and plans of action and milestones (POA&M) for implementing security controls. Procedures should be in place outlining who reviews the plans, keeps the plan current, and follows up on planned security controls. In addition, procedures should require that system security plans be developed and reviewed prior to proceeding with the security certification and accreditation process for the system.

During the security certification and accreditation process, the system security plan is analyzed, updated, and accepted. The certification agent confirms that the security controls described in the system security plan are consistent with the FIPS 199 security category determined for the information system, and that the threat and vulnerability identification and initial risk determination is identified and documented in the system security plan, risk assessment, or equivalent document. The results of a security certification are used to reassess the risks, develop the POA&Ms that are required to track remedial actions, and update the system security plan, thus providing the factual basis for an authorizing official to render a security accreditation decision.[53]

The roles and responsibilities in this section are specific to information system security planning. Recognizing that agencies have widely varying missions and organizational structures, there may be differences in naming conventions for security planning-related roles and how the associated responsibilities are allocated among agency personnel (e.g., multiple individuals filling a single role or one individual filling multiple roles).[54,55]

8.2.1 Chief Information Officer

The chief information officer (CIO)[56] is the agency official responsible for developing and maintaining an agency-wide information security program and has the following system security planning responsibilities:

---

[52] NIST SP 800-37 defines a minor application as an application, other than major application, that requires attention to security due to the risk and magnitude of harm resulting from the loss, misuse, or unauthorized access to or modification of the information in the application. Minor applications are typically included as part of a GSS.

[53] See NIST SP 800-37, *Guide for the Security Certification and Accreditation of Federal Information Systems*, and Chapter 11, Certification and Accreditation, of this guide for additional guidance on the C&A process.

[54] Caution should be exercised when one individual fills multiple roles in the security planning process to ensure that the individual retains an appropriate level of independence and remains free from conflicts of interest.

[55] See Chapter 2, Governance, Chapter 5, Capital Planning, Chapter 11, Certification, Accreditation, and Security Assessments, and Chapter 14, Configuration Management, of this guide for additional guidance on roles and responsibilities.

[56] When an agency has not designated a formal CIO position, the Federal Information Security Management Act (FISMA) requires the associated responsibilities to be handled by a comparable agency official.

- Designating an SAISO who shall carry out the CIO's responsibilities for system security planning;
- Developing and maintaining information security policies, procedures, and control techniques to address system security planning;
- Managing the identification, implementation, and assessment of common security controls;
- Ensuring that personnel with significant responsibilities for system security plans are trained;
- Assisting senior agency officials with their responsibilities for system security plans; and
- Identifying and developing common security controls for the agency.

8.2.2 Information System Owner

The information system owner[57] is the agency official responsible for the overall procurement, development, integration, modification, and operation and maintenance of the information system. The information system owner has the following responsibilities related to system security plans:

- Developing the system security plan in coordination with information owners, the system administrator, the information system security officer (ISSO), the SAISO, and functional "end users";
- Maintaining the system security plan and ensuring that the system is deployed and operated according to the agreed-upon security requirements; and
- Ensuring that system users and support personnel receive the requisite security training (e.g., instruction in rules of behavior) and assisting in the identification, implementation, and assessment of the common security controls.

8.2.3 Information Owner

The information owner is the agency official with statutory or operational authority for specified information and is responsible for establishing the controls for information generation, collection, processing, dissemination, and disposal. The information owner has the following responsibilities related to system security plans:

- Establishing the rules for the appropriate use and protection of the subject data/information (rules of behavior);[58]
- Providing input to information system owners on the security requirements and security controls for the information systems where the information resides;
- Deciding who has access to the information system and determining what types of privileges or access rights; and
- Assisting in identifying and assessing the common security controls where the information resides.

---

[57] The role of the information system owner can be interpreted in a variety of ways depending on the particular agency and the SDLC phase of the information system. Some agencies may refer to information system owners as program managers or business/asset/mission owners.

[58] The information owner retains that responsibility even when the data/information is shared with other organizations.

8.2.4 Senior Agency Information Security Officer

The SAISO is the agency official responsible for serving as the CIO's primary liaison to the agency's information system owners and ISSOs. The SAISO has the following responsibilities related to system security plans:

- Carrying out the CIO's responsibilities for system security planning;

- Coordinating the development, review, and acceptance of system security plans with information system owners, ISSOs, and the authorizing official;

- Coordinating the identification, implementation, and assessment of the common security controls; and

- Possessing professional qualifications, including training and experience, required to develop and review system security plans.

8.2.5 Information System Security Officer

The ISSO is the agency official assigned responsibility by the SAISO, authorizing official, management official, or information system owner for ensuring that the appropriate operational security posture is maintained for an information system or program. The ISSO has the following responsibilities related to system security plans:

- Assisting the SAISO in identifying, implementing, and assessing the common security controls; and

- Actively supporting the development and maintenance of the system security plan, to include coordinating system changes with the information system owner and assessing the security impact of those changes.

8.3 Rules of Behavior

The rules of behavior, which are required in OMB Circular A-130, Appendix III, and are also a form of security control found in NIST SP 800-53, should clearly delineate responsibilities and expected behavior of all individuals with access to the system. The rules should state the consequences of inconsistent behavior or noncompliance and be made available to every user prior to receiving authorization for system access. It is required that the rules contain a signature page for each user to acknowledge receipt, indicating that they have read, understand, and agree to abide by the rules of behavior. Electronic signatures are acceptable for use in acknowledging the rules of behavior.

Table 8-1 lists examples from OMB Circular A-130, Appendix III, of what should be covered in typical rules of behavior. These are examples only and agencies have flexibility in the detail and content. When developing the rules of behavior, agencies should be aware that the intended function of this document is to make all users accountable for their actions by acknowledging that they have read, understood, and agreed to abide by the rules of behavior. The rules, while not intended as a complete copy of the security policy or procedures guide, should cover, at a high level, some of the controls described in Table 8-1. Lastly, agencies can incorporate, by reference, the agency body of policies and procedures governing information security and other applicable policies in the text of the rules of behavior.

Table 8-1. Rules of Behavior Examples

Examples of Controls Contained in Rules of Behavior

<ul><li>Delineate responsibilities, expected use of system, and behavior of all users</li><li>Describe appropriate limits on interconnections</li><li>Define service provisions and restoration priorities</li><li>Be clear on consequences of behavior not consistent with rules</li><li>Covers the following topics:
   – Work at home   – Unofficial use of government equipment
   – Dial-in access   – Assignment and limitations of system privileges and individual accountability
   – Connection to the Internet   – Password usage
   – Use of copyrighted work   – Searching databases and divulging information</li></ul>

8.4 System Security Plan Approval

Organizational policy should clearly define who is responsible for system security plan approval and procedures developed for plan submission, including any special memorandum language or other documentation required by the agency. Prior to the security certification and accreditation process, the authorizing official, independent from the system owner, typically approves the plan.

8.4.1 System Boundary Analysis and Security Controls

Before the system security plan can be developed, the information system and the information resident within that system must be categorized based on a FIPS 199 impact analysis.[59] Then a determination can be made as to which systems in the inventory can be logically grouped into GSSs or MAs. The FIPS 199 impact levels must be considered when the system boundaries are drawn and when selecting the initial set of security controls (e.g., control baseline). The baseline security controls can then be tailored based on an assessment of risk and local conditions, including organization-specific security requirements, specific threat information, cost-benefit analyses, the availability of compensating controls, or special circumstances. Common security controls, which is one of the tailoring considerations, must be identified prior to system security plan preparation to identify those controls covered at the agency level that are not system-specific. These common security controls can then be incorporated into the system security plan by reference. Figure 8-1 depicts how large GSSs can be broken down for the purpose of security planning.

The process of uniquely assigning information resources[60] to an information system defines the security boundary for that system. Agencies have great flexibility in determining what constitutes an information system (i.e., MA or GSS). If a set of information resources is identified as an information system, the resources should generally be under the same direct management control. Direct management control[61] does not necessarily imply that there is no intervening management. It is also possible for an information system to contain multiple *subsystems*. A subsystem is a major subdivision or component of an information system consisting of information, information technology (IT), and personnel that perform one or more specific functions.

---

[59] See NIST SP 800-60, *Guide for Mapping Types of Information and Information Systems to Security Categories*, for supporting guidance on system categorization.

[60] Information resources consist of information and related resources such as personnel, equipment, funds, and information technology.

[61] Direct management control typically involves budgetary, programmatic, or operational authority and associated responsibility. For new information systems, management control can be interpreted as having budgetary/programmatic authority and responsibility for developing and deploying the information systems. For information systems currently in the federal inventory, management control can be interpreted as having budgetary/operational authority for the day-to-day operation and maintenance of the information systems.

8.4.2 Security Controls

FIPS 200 provides seventeen minimum security requirements for federal information and information systems. The requirements represent a broad-based, balanced information security program that addresses the management, operational, and technical aspects of protecting the confidentiality, integrity, and availability of federal information and information systems. An agency must meet the minimum security requirements in this standard by applying security controls selected in accordance with NIST SP 800-53 and the designated impact levels of the information systems. An agency has the flexibility to tailor the security control baseline in accordance with the terms and conditions set forth in the standard. Tailoring activities include (1) the application of scoping guidance, (2) the specification of compensating controls, and (3) the specification of agency-defined parameters in the security controls, where allowed. The system security plan should document all tailoring activities.

8.4.3 Scoping Guidance

Subsystems typically fall under the same management authority and are included within a single system security plan. Figure 8-1 depicted a GSS with three subsystems. Scoping guidance provides an agency with specific terms and conditions on the applicability and implementation of individual security controls in the security control baselines defined in NIST SP 800-53. Several considerations described below can potentially impact how the baseline security controls are applied by the agency. System security plans should clearly identify which security controls used scoping guidance and include a description of the type of considerations that were made. The application of scoping guidance must be reviewed and approved by the authorizing official for the information system.

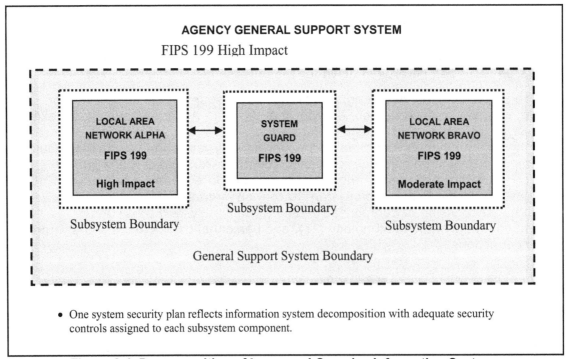

Figure 8-1. Decomposition of Large and Complex Information Systems

8.4.4 Compensating Controls

Compensating security controls are the management, operational, or technical controls used by an agency in lieu of prescribed controls in the low, moderate, or high security control baselines, which provide equivalent or comparable protection for an information system. Compensating security controls for an information system will be used by an agency only under the following conditions: (1) the agency selects the compensating controls from the security control catalog in NIST SP 800-53, (2) the agency provides a complete and convincing rationale and justification for how the compensating controls provide an equivalent security capability or level of protection for the information system, and (3) the agency assesses and formally accepts the risk associated with using the compensating controls in the information system. The use of compensating security controls must be reviewed, documented in the system security plan, and approved by the authorizing official for the information system.

8.4.5 Common Security Controls

An agency-wide view of the information security program facilitates the identification of common security controls that can be applied to one or more agency information systems. Common security controls can apply to (1) all agency information systems; (2) a group of information systems at a specific site (sometimes associated with the term site certification/accreditation); or (3) common information systems, subsystems, or applications (i.e., common hardware, software, and/or firmware) deployed at multiple operational sites (sometimes associated with the term type certification/accreditation). Common security controls—typically identified during a collaborative agency-wide process that involves the CIO, SAISO, authorizing officials, information system owners, and ISSOs (and by developmental program managers in the case of common security controls for common hardware, software, and/or firmware)—have the following properties:

- The development, implementation, and assessment of common security controls can be assigned to responsible agency officials or organizational elements (other than the information system owners whose systems will implement or use those common security controls).

- The results from the assessment of the common security controls can be used to support the security certification and accreditation processes of agency information systems where those controls have been applied.

For efficiency in developing system security plans, common security controls should be documented once and then inserted or imported into each system security plan for the information systems within the agency. Effectively maximizing the application of common controls in the system security planning process depends on the following factors:

- The agency has developed, documented, and communicated its specific guidance on identifying common security controls.

- The agency has assigned the responsibility for coordinating common security control identification and review and obtaining consensus on the common control designations with a management official, such as the CIO or SAISO, with security program responsibilities.

- System owners have been briefed on the system security planning process, including use of common controls.

- Agency experts in the common control areas identified have been consulted as part of the process.

While the concept of security control partitioning into common security controls and system-specific controls is straightforward and intuitive, the application of this principle within an agency takes planning, coordination, and perseverance. If an agency is just beginning to implement this approach or has only partially implemented this approach, it may take some time to get the maximum benefits from security control partitioning and the associated reuse of assessment evidence. Because of the potential dependence on common security controls by many of an agency's information systems, a failure of such common controls may result in a significant increase in agency-level risk—risk that arises from operating the systems that depend on these security controls.

8.5 Security Control Selection

An agency must meet the minimum security requirements in FIPS 199 by selecting the appropriate security controls and assurance requirements as described in NIST SP 800-53. The process of selecting the appropriate security controls and assurance requirements for agency information systems to achieve *adequate security*[62] is a multifaceted, risk-based activity involving management and operational personnel within the agency. Security categorization of federal information and information systems, as required by FIPS 199, is the first step in the risk management process.[63] Subsequent to the security categorization process, an agency must select an appropriate set of security controls for their information systems that satisfy the minimum security requirements set forth in FIPS 200. The selected set of security controls must be one of three security control baselines from NIST SP 800-53 (see Table 8-2) that are associated with the designated impact levels of the agency information systems as determined during the security categorization process.

- For *low-impact* information systems, an agency must, at a minimum, use the security controls from the low baseline of security controls defined in NIST SP 800-53 and must ensure that the minimum assurance requirements associated with the low baseline are satisfied.

- For *moderate-impact* information systems, an agency must, at a minimum, employ the security controls from the moderate baseline of security controls defined in NIST SP 800-53 and must ensure that the minimum assurance requirements associated with the moderate baseline are satisfied.

- For *high-impact* information systems, an agency must, at a minimum, use the security controls from the high baseline of security controls defined in NIST SP 800-53 and must ensure that the minimum assurance requirements associated with the high baseline are satisfied.

---

[62] OMB Circular A-130, Appendix III, defines adequate security as security commensurate with the risk and the magnitude of harm resulting from the loss, misuse, or unauthorized access to or modification of information.

[63] Security categorization must be accomplished as an enterprise-wide activity with the involvement of senior-level organizational officials including, but not limited to, CIOs, SAISOs, authorizing officials (also known as accreditation authorities), information system owners, and information owners. NIST SP 800-60 provides implementation guidance for FIPS 199.

Table 8-2. FIPS 199 Categorization

Security Objective	Potential Impact		
	Low	**Moderate**	**High**
Confidentiality Preserving authorized restrictions on information access and disclosure, including means for protecting personal privacy and proprietary information. [44 U.S.C., SEC. 3542]	The unauthorized disclosure of information could be expected to have a **limited** adverse effect on organizational operations, organizational assets, or individuals.	The unauthorized disclosure of information could be expected to have a **serious** adverse effect on organizational operations, organizational assets, or individuals.	The unauthorized disclosure of information could be expected to have a **severe or catastrophic** adverse effect on organizational operations, organizational assets, or individuals.
Integrity Guarding against improper information modification or destruction, and includes ensuring information non-repudiation and authenticity. [44 U.S.C., SEC. 3542]	The unauthorized modification or destruction of information could be expected to have a **limited** adverse effect on organizational operations, organizational assets, or individuals.	The unauthorized modification or destruction of information could be expected to have a **serious** adverse effect on organizational operations, organizational assets, or individuals.	The unauthorized modification or destruction of information could be expected to have a **severe or catastrophic** adverse effect on organizational operations, organizational assets, or individuals.
Availability Ensuring timely and reliable access to and use of information. [44 U.S.C., SEC. 3542]	The disruption of access to or use of information or an information system could be expected to have a **limited** adverse effect on organizational operations, organizational assets, or individuals.	The disruption of access to or use of information or an information system could be expected to have a **serious** adverse effect on organizational operations, organizational assets, or individuals.	The disruption of access to or use of information or an information system could be expected to have a **severe or catastrophic** adverse effect on organizational operations, organizational assets, or individuals.

8.6 Completion and Approval Dates

The completion date of the system security plan should be provided. The completion date should be updated whenever the plan is periodically reviewed and updated. The system security plan should also contain the date the authorizing official or the designated approving authority approves the plan. Approval documentation, e.g., accreditation letter, should be on file or attached as part of the plan.

8.7 Ongoing System Security Plan Maintenance

Once the information system security plan is accredited, it is important to periodically assess the plan; review any change in system status, functionality, design, etc.; and ensure that the plan continues to reflect the correct information about the system. This documentation and its accuracy are imperative for system recertification and reaccreditation activity. All plans should be reviewed and updated, if appropriate, at least annually. Some items to include in the review are:

- Change in information system owner;
- Change in information security representative;
- Major change in system architecture;
- Change in system status;
- Additions/deletions of system interconnections;
- Change in system scope; and
- Change in authorizing official.

The objective of system security planning is to improve the protection of information system resources. All federal systems have some level of sensitivity and require protection as part of good management practice. The protection of a system must be documented in a system security plan. The completion of system security plans is a requirement of the OMB Circular A-130, *Management of Federal Information Resources,* Appendix III, *Security of Federal Automated Information Resources*, and Title III of the E-Government Act, FISMA.

For the plans to adequately reflect the protection of the resources, a senior management official must authorize a system to process information or operate. This authorization provides an important quality control. By authorizing processing in a system, the manager accepts its associated risk.

Management authorization should be based on an assessment of management, operational, and technical controls. Since the system security plan establishes and documents the security controls, it should form the basis for the authorization, supplemented by the assessment report and the POA&Ms. In addition, a periodic review of controls should also contribute to future authorizations. Reauthorization should occur prior to a significant change in processing, but at least every three years.

Website:
www.csrc.nist.gov

References:
Public Law 107-347 [H.R. 2458], *The E-Government Act of 2002, Title III of this Act is the Federal Information Security Management Act of 2002 (FISMA)*, December 17, 2002.

Office of Management and Budget Circular A-130, *Management of Federal Information Resources*, November 2000.

Federal Information Processing Standard 199, *Standards for Security Categorization of Federal Information and Information Systems*, February 2004.

Federal Information Processing Standard 200, *Minimum Security Requirements for Federal Information and Information Systems,* March 2006.

National Institute of Standards and Technology Special Publication 800-18, Revision 1, *Guide for Developing Security Plans for Federal Information Systems,* February 2006.

National Institute of Standards and Technology Special Publication 800-30, *Risk Management Guide for Information Technology Systems*, July 2002.

National Institute of Standards and Technology Special Publication 800-37, *Guide for the Security Certification and Accreditation of Federal Information Systems*, May 2004.

National Institute of Standards and Technology Special Publication 800-53, Revision 1, *Recommended Security Controls for Federal Information System,* February 2006.

National Institute of Standards and Technology Special Publication 800-60, *Guide for Mapping Types of Information and Information Systems to Security Categories*, June 2004.

National Institute of Standards and Technology Special Publication 800-64, *Security Considerations in the Information System Development Life Cycle*, Rev. 1 June 2004.

Chapter 9

9. Information Technology Contingency Planning

Information technology (IT) contingency planning is one modular piece of a larger contingency and continuity of operations (COOP) planning process that encompasses IT, business processes, risk management, financial management, crisis communications, safety and security of personnel and property, and continuity of government. Each piece is operative in its own right, but in concert creates synergy that efficiently and effectively protects the entire organization.[64]

Contingency planning for information systems is a required process for developing general support systems (GSS) and major applications (MA) with appropriate backup methods and procedures for implementing data recovery and reconstitution against IT risks.[65] Risks to information systems may be natural, technological, or human in nature. Contingency planning consists of a *process* for recovery and documentation of *procedures* for conducting recovery. National Institute of Standards and Technology (NIST) Special Publication (SP) 800-34, *Contingency Planning for Information Technology Systems*, details a seven-step methodology for developing an IT contingency process and plan. Planning, implementing, and testing the contingency strategy are addressed by six of the seven steps; documenting the plan and establishing procedures and personnel organization to implement the strategy is the final step. SP 800-34 also includes technical considerations for developing recovery strategies.

Figure 9-1 highlights contingency planning activities involved in each step that should be addressed during all phases of the system development life cycle (SDLC).[66]

The capability to recover and reconstitute data should be integral to the information system design concept during the Initiation phase. Recovery strategies should be built into the GSS or MA's architecture during the Development phase. The contingency processes should be tested and maintained during the Implementation phase; contingency plans should be exercised and maintained during the Operations/Maintenance phase. When the information system has reached the Disposal phase, the legacy system should remain intact and operational as a contingency to the replaced information system until, at least, the new system has been sufficiently tested. At some point, the legacy system may no longer support the needs of the organization, and the recovery strategy may transition away from the legacy system to a new recovery strategy designed during the Development phase of the new system.

---

[64] All departments and agencies must have IT contingency plans for certified and accredited systems and must also have an organizational Continuity of Operations (COOP) plan for essential federal functions.

[65] See NIST FIPS 199, *Standards for Security Categorization of Federal Information and Information Systems,* NIST 800-60, *Guide for Mapping Types of Information and Information Systems to Security Categories,* and Chapter 8, Security Planning, of this guide for additional guidance on determining system classifications.

[66] See National Institute of Standards and Technology Special Publication 800-64, *Security Considerations in the Information System Development Life Cycle,* and Chapter 3, System Development Life Cycle, of this guide for additional guidance on the SDLC.

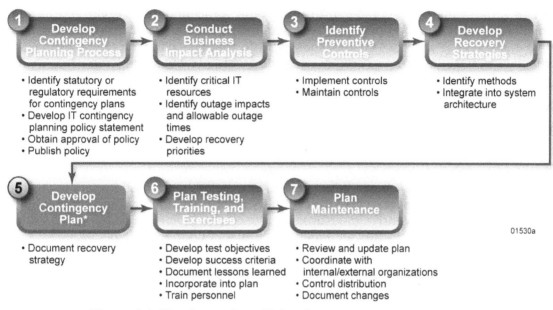

Figure 9-1. The Seven-Step IT Contingency Planning Process

9.1 Step 1: Develop Contingency Planning Policy Statement

When developing an IT contingency plan, the first step is to establish a contingency planning policy within the organization. This policy may exist at the department, agency, and/or program level of the organization. The statement should define the organization's overall contingency objectives; identify leadership, roles and responsibilities, resource requirements, test, training, and exercise schedules; and develop maintenance schedules and determine the minimum required backup frequency.

9.2 Step 2: Conduct Business Impact Analysis

A business impact analysis (BIA) is a critical step to understanding the information systems components, interdependencies, and potential downtime impacts. Contingency plan strategy and procedures should be designed in consideration of the results of the BIA.

> **BIA Critical Resource Example**
>
> *Time and attendance reporting may require use of a local area network (LAN) server, wide area network (WAN) access, e-mail, and an e-mail server.*

A BIA is conducted by identifying the system's critical resources. Each critical resource is then further examined to determine how long functionality of the resource could be withheld from the information system before an unacceptable impact is experienced.

> **BIA Resource Impact Example**
>
> *LAN disruption to the time and attendance reporting system for 8 hours may create a delay in time sheet processing.*

The impact may be something that materializes over time or may be tracked across related resources and dependent systems (e.g., cascading domino effect). The time identified is called a maximum allowable outage (MAO). Based on the potential impacts, the amount of time the information system

> **BIA Recovery Time Objective Example**
>
> *The LAN server must be recovered within 8 hours to avoid a delay in time sheet processing.*

can be without the critical resource then provides a recourse recovery priority around which an organization can plan recovery activities. The balancing point between the MAO and the cost to recover establishes the information system's recovery time objective (RTO). Recovery strategies must be created to meet the RTO.

The strategy must also address recovering information system critical components within a priority, as established by their individual RTOs.

9.3 Step 3: Identify Preventive Controls

In some cases, implementing preventive controls might mitigate outage impacts identified by the BIA. Preventive controls are measures that detect, deter, and/or reduce impacts to the system. When cost-effective, preventing an impact is desired over implementing recovery strategies (and therefore risking data loss and impact to the organization). Preventive measures are specific to individual components and the environment in which the components operate. Common controls include:

- Uninterruptible power supply (UPS);
- Fire suppression systems;
- Gasoline or diesel-powered generators;
- Air conditioning systems with excess capacity to permit failure of certain components;
- Heat-resistant and waterproof containers for backup media and vital
- nonelectronic records; and
- Frequent, scheduled data backups.

9.4 Step 4: Develop Recovery Strategies

When a disruption occurs despite the preventive measures implemented, a recovery strategy must be in place to recover and restore data and system operations

> ### *Recovery Strategy Tip*
> *The chosen strategy must also be coordinated with the IT contingency plans of interdependent systems and business continuity plans of interdependent business processes.*

within the RTO period. The recovery strategy is designed from a combination of methods, which together address the full spectrum of information system risks. Several options may be evaluated during the Development phase; the most cost-effective option, based on potential impact, should be selected and integrated into the information system architecture and operating procedures.

System data must be backed up regularly; therefore, all IT contingency plans should include a method and frequency for conducting data backups.

> ### *Recovery Strategy Tip*
> *Stored data should be routinely tested to validate backed-up data integrity.*

The frequency of backup methods—daily or weekly, incremental or full—should be selected based on system criticality when new information is introduced. The backup method selected should be based on system and data availability and integrity requirements (as defined in the BIA). Data that is backed up may need to be stored offsite and rotated frequently, depending upon the criticality of the system.

Major disruptions to system operations may require restoration activities to be implemented at an alternate site. The type of alternate site selected must be based on RTO requirements and budget limitations. Equipment for recovering and/or replacing the information system must be provided as part of the recovery strategy. Cost, delivery time, and compatibility factors must also be considered when determining how to provide the necessary equipment. Agencies must also plan for an alternate site that, at a minimum, provides workspace for all contingency plan personnel, equipment, and the appropriate IT infrastructure necessary to execute IT contingency plan and system recovery activities.

The level of operational readiness of the alternate site is an important characteristic to determine when developing the recovery strategy. NIST SP 800-34 provides an overview of the common types of alternate sites.

The recovery strategy requires personnel to implement the procedures and test operability. Generally, a member of the organization's senior leadership is selected to activate the plan and lead overall recovery operations. Appropriate teams of personnel (at least two people to ensure there is a primary and alternate available to execute procedures) are identified to be responsible for specific aspects of the plan.

Personnel should be chosen to staff the teams based on their normal responsibilities, system knowledge, and availability to recover the system on an on-call basis. A line of succession should be defined to ensure that someone can assume the role of senior leadership if the plan leader is unable to respond.

Having selected choices for each component of the recovery strategy, the final consideration should be given to cost. The recovery strategy must meet criticality, availability, and RTO requirements while remaining within budget. Less obvious costs—such as shipping, awareness programs, tests and exercises, travel, labor hours, and contracted services—must also be incorporated into the evaluation.

9.5 Step 5: Develop IT Contingency Plan

Procedures for executing the recovery strategy are outlined in the IT contingency plan. The plan must be written in a format that will provide the users (recovery team leadership and members) the context in which the plan is to be implemented and the direct procedures, based on role, to execute. IT contingency plans are constructed using five components as depicted in Figure 9-2.

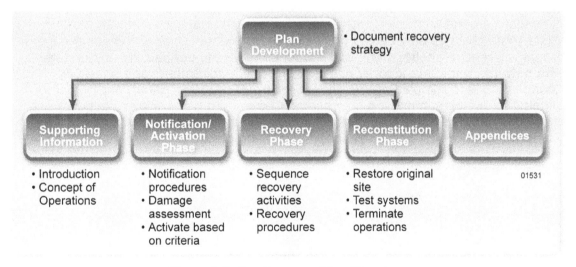

Figure 9-2. Contingency Plan Structure

The procedures are documented in the Notification/Activation Phase, Recovery Phase, and Reconstitution Phase components of the plan. The Supporting Information and Appendices components provide supplemental information necessary to understand the context in which the plan is to be used and gives additional information that may be necessary to execute procedures (e.g., emergency contact information and the BIA).

9.6 Step 6: Plan Testing, Training, and Exercises

Personnel selected to execute the IT contingency plan must be trained to perform the procedures, the plan must be exercised, and the system strategy must be tested.

Plan testing should include:

- System recovery on an alternate platform from backup media
- Coordination among recovery teams
- Internal and external connectivity
- System performance using alternate equipment
- Restoration of normal operations
- Notification procedures.

Personnel training should include:

- Purpose of the plan
- Cross-team coordination and communication
- Reporting procedures
- Security requirements
- Team-specific processes
- Individual responsibilities.

Plan exercises should be designed to individually and then collectively examine various components of the entire plan. Exercises may be conducted in a classroom setting: discussing specific components of the plan and/or impact issues; or they may be functional exercises: simulating the recovery using actual replacement equipment, data, and alternate sites.

9.7   Step 7: Plan Maintenance

The IT contingency plan must always be maintained in a ready state for use immediately upon notification. Periodic reviews of the plan must be conducted for currency of key personnel and vendor information, system components and dependencies, the recovery strategy, vital records, and operational requirements. While some changes may be obvious (e.g., personnel turnover or vendor changes), others will require analysis. The BIA should be reviewed periodically and updated with new information to identify new contingency requirements and priorities. Changes made to the plan are noted in a record of changes, dated, and signed or initialed by the person making the change. The revised plan, or plan sections, are circulated to those with plan responsibilities. Because of the impact that plan changes may have on interdependent business processes or information systems, the changes must be clearly communicated and properly annotated in the beginning of the document.

Websites:
Federal Emergency Management Agency (FEMA)
http://www.FEMA.gov
www.csrc.nist.gov

References:

Federal Information Processing Standard 199, *Standards for Security Categorization of Federal Information and Information Systems*, February 2004.

National Institute of Standards and Technology Special Publication 800-30, *Risk Management Guide for Information Technology Systems*, July 2002.

National Institute of Standards and Technology Special Publication 800-34, *Contingency Planning Guide for Information Technology Systems*, June 2002.

National Institute of Standards and Technology Special Publication 800-60, *Guide for Mapping Types of Information and Information Systems to Security Categories*, June 2004.

National Institute of Standards and Technology Special Publication 800-64, *Security Considerations in the Information System Development Life Cycle*, Rev. 1 June 2004.

Chapter 10

10. Risk Management

An effective risk management process is an important component of a successful information security program. The principal goal of an organization's risk management process is to protect the organization and its ability to perform its mission, not just its information assets. Therefore, the risk management process should not be treated primarily as a technical function carried out by the information security experts who operate and manage the information security system, but as an essential management function of the organization that is tightly woven into the system development life cycle (SDLC), [67] as depicted in Figure 10-1. Because risk cannot be eliminated entirely, the risk management process allows information security program managers to balance the operational and economic costs of protective measures and achieve gains in mission capability. By employing practices and procedures designed to foster informed decision making, agencies help protect their information systems and the data that support their own mission.

Figure 10-1. Risk Management in the System Security Life Cycle

---

[67] See National Institute of Standards and Technology (NIST) Special Publication (SP) 800-64, *Security Considerations in the Information System Development Life Cycle*, and Chapter 3, System Development Life Cycle, of this guide for additional information on the SDLC.

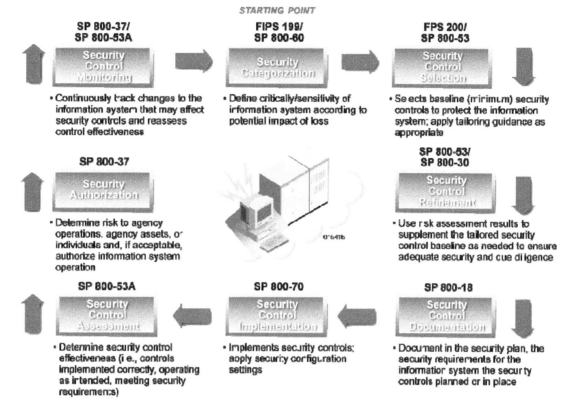

Risk management is an aggregation of three processes that have their roots in several federal laws, regulations, and guidelines, including the Computer Security Act of 1987, the Federal Information Security Management Act (FISMA), Office of Management and Budget (OMB) Circular A-130, and National Institute of Standards and Technology (NIST) Special Publication (SP) 800-30, *Risk Management Guide for Information Technology Systems*. The three processes are risk assessment, risk mitigation, and evaluation and assessment. If applied appropriately and with due diligence, this process meets the FISMA requirements of "providing information security protections commensurate with the risk and magnitude of the harm resulting from unauthorized access, use, disclosure, disruption, modification, or destruction of…information…and…information systems" collected by and used by the federal government, and "ensuring that information security management processes are integrated with agency strategic and operational planning processes."

10.1 Risk Assessment

To understand the risk assessment process, it is essential to define the term risk. NIST SP 800-30 defines risk as "a function of the likelihood of a given threat source's exercising a particular potential vulnerability, and the resulting impact of that adverse event on the organization." In other words, where a threat intersects with a vulnerability, risk is present. With this definition of risk in mind, the goal of the risk assessment process is to identify and assess the risks to a given environment. The depth of the risk assessment performed can vary greatly and is determined by the criticality and sensitivity of the system, as applied to confidentiality, integrity, and availability, a process which is described in detail in Federal Information Processing Standard (FIPS) 199. To meet the goal of the risk assessment, a nine-step process is defined in NIST SP 800-30 and summarized here. To simplify the process somewhat, the nine-step process described in NIST SP 800-30 is reduced to a six-

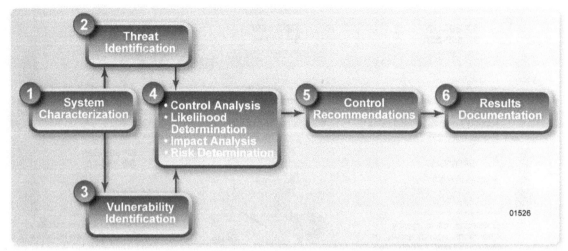

Figure 10-3. Risk Assessment Process

step process, whereby Steps 4, 5, and 6 of the process are combined to create the Risk Analysis step (see Figures 10-2 and 10-3). Depicted in Figure 10-2, below, is a high-level depiction of risk assessment process.

The likelihood of a given threat successfully exploiting a given vulnerability is estimated by evaluating the threat source's motivation, opportunity, and methods for conducting such an exploitation. The impact of a successful exploitation is estimated through an analysis of the effect the exploitation can have on the confidentiality, integrity, and availability of the system and the data it processes. The determination of the criticality and sensitivity of the system, in terms of its confidentiality, integrity, and availability, is found by applying the concepts and processes discussed in detail within FIPS 199, *Standards for Security Categorization of Federal Information and Information Systems*.

As mandated by OMB Circular A-130, the risk assessment process is usually repeated at least every three years for federal agencies. However, risk assessments should be conducted and integrated into the SDLC for information systems, not because it is required by law or regulation, but because it is a good practice and supports the organization's business objectives or mission.

10.1.1 Step 1 – System Characterization

Characterizing an information system establishes the scope of the risk assessment effort, delineates the operational authorization (or accreditation) boundaries, and provides information (e.g., hardware, software, system connectivity, and responsible division or support personnel). This step begins with the identification of the information system boundaries, resources, and information.

When characterizing the system, the mission criticality and sensitivity (as previously identified using FIPS 199 to determine the system's appropriate security categorization) are described in sufficient terms to form a basis for the scope of the risk assessment. The level of effort and the granularity (i.e., the level of depth to which the assessment investigates the security of the system) of the risk assessment are based on the FIPS 199 security categorization. For example, a system determined to be of low impact may not require hands-on security testing and evaluation. Various techniques, such as questionnaires, interviews, documentation reviews, and automated scanning tools, can be used to collect the information needed to fully characterize the system. At a minimum, the system characterization describes the following individual system components:

- Hardware (e.g., IBM mainframe running the z/OS operating system, Dell server running Windows 2003);
- Software (e.g., Oracle, Apache web server, Microsoft Internet Information Server [IIS]);
- External interfaces to other systems;
- Data; and
- People.

In addition to the component descriptions, the system characterization describes other factors with the potential to affect the security of the system, such as:

- System functional requirements;
- Organizational security policy and architecture;
- System network topology;
- Information flows throughout the system;
- Management, operational, and technical security controls implemented or planned to be implemented for the system; and
- Physical and environmental security mechanisms.

The accuracy of the results from this step is essential to obtaining the best view of the risk profile of the system undergoing assessment, since this step provides the basis for the remaining steps. Inaccuracy at this point will propagate and lead to a cascade of analytical errors as the process progresses.

10.1.2 Step 2 – Threat Identification

Threat identification consists of identifying threat sources with the potential to exploit weaknesses in the system. This step should culminate in the development of a "threat statement," or a comprehensive listing of potential threat sources. The threat statement must be tailored to the individual organization and its processing environment (e.g., end-user computing habits), which is accomplished by performing a threat evaluation, using the system characterization as the basis, for the potential to cause harm to the system.

There are common threat sources that typically apply, regardless of the system, that should be evaluated. These common threats can be categorized into three areas: (1) natural threats (e.g., floods, earthquakes, tornadoes, landslides, avalanches, electrical storms), (2) human threats (intentional or unintentional), and (3) environmental threats (e.g., power failure). In general, information on natural threats (e.g., floods, earthquakes, storms) should be readily available, as known threats have been identified by many government and private sector organizations. Intrusion detection tools also are becoming more prevalent, and government and industry organizations continually collect data on security events, thereby improving the ability to realistically assess threats. Sources of information include, but are not limited to, the following:

- Intelligence agencies (for example, the Federal Bureau of Investigation's National Infrastructure Protection Center);
- United States Computer Emergency Readiness Team (US-CERT) found at www.us-cert.gov); and
- Mass media, including Web-based resources.

10.1.3 Step 3 – Vulnerability Identification

NIST SP 800-30 defines vulnerability as "a flaw or weakness in system security procedures, design, implementation, or internal controls that could be exercised (accidentally triggered or intentionally exploited) and result in a security breach or a violation of the system's security policy." Vulnerabilities can be identified using a combination of a number of techniques and sources. Reviews of such sources as previous risk assessments, audit reports, vulnerability lists [e.g., NIST National Vulnerability Database (NVD), formerly known as I-CAT, found at nvd.nist.gov], and security advisories can be used to begin the process of vulnerability identification. System security testing, using methods such as automated vulnerability scanning tools; security, test, and evaluation (ST&E); and penetration testing can be used to augment the vulnerability source reviews and identify vulnerabilities that may not have been previously identified in other sources.

In addition, developing a security requirements checklist based on the security requirements specified for the system during the conceptual, design, and implementation phases of the SDLC can be used to provide a 360-degree inspection of the system. The checklist can be developed using the guidance provided in NIST SP 800-53A, *Guide for Assessing the Security Controls in Federal Information Systems (draft)*, and NIST SP 800-53, *Recommended Security Controls for Federal Information Systems*, to ensure the inclusion of appropriate questions in the areas of management, operational, and technical security controls. The results of the checklist (or questionnaire) can be used as input for evaluating compliance and noncompliance, which in turn identifies system, process, and procedural weaknesses that represent potential vulnerabilities.

10.1.4 Step 4 – Risk Analysis

The risk analysis is a determination (or estimation) of risk to the system, an analysis that requires the consideration of closely interwoven factors, such as the security controls in place for the system under review, the likelihood that those controls will be either insufficient or ineffective protection of the system, and the impact of that failure. In other words, it is not possible to estimate the level of risk posed by the successful exploitation of a given vulnerability without considering the efficacy of the security controls that have been or are to be implemented to mitigate or eliminate the potential for such an exploitation; nor the threat's motivation, opportunity, and capabilities, which contribute to the likelihood of a successful attack; nor the impact to the system and organization should successful exploitation of a vulnerability occur. The following four steps—control analysis, likelihood determination, impact analysis, and risk determination—are, in a practical sense, performed simultaneously or nearly simultaneously because they are so tightly linked to each other.

10.1.4.1 Control Analysis

As previously discussed, the analysis of controls in place to protect the system can be accomplished using a checklist or questionnaire, which is based on the security requirements for the system as specified by NIST SP 800-53. This analysis can be refined using the NIST SP 800-53A, *Guide for Assessing the Security Controls in Federal Information Systems (draft)*, which provides guidance on testing security controls extracted from NIST SP 800-53. The results are used to strengthen the determination of the likelihood that a specific threat might successfully exploit a particular vulnerability.

10.1.4.2   Likelihood Determination

Likelihood determination considers a threat source's motivation and capability to exploit a vulnerability, the nature of the vulnerability, the existence of security controls, and the effectiveness of mitigating security controls. Likelihood ratings are described in the qualitative terms of high, moderate, and low, and are used to describe how likely is a successful exploitation of a vulnerability by a given threat. For example, if a threat is highly motivated and sufficiently capable, and controls implemented to protect the vulnerability are ineffective, then it is highly likely that the attack would be successful. In this scenario, the appropriate likelihood rating would be high. The likelihood ratings of moderate and low are similarly defined to successively lesser degrees.

10.1.4.3   Impact Analysis

The third factor used in determining the level of risk to a system is impact. A proper overall impact analysis considers the following factors: impact to the systems, data, and the organization's mission. Additionally, this analysis should also consider the criticality and sensitivity of the system and its data. FIPS 199 provides a consistent, focused process for categorizing a system's criticality and sensitivity for the three security domains of confidentiality, integrity, and availability. Using FIPS 199 to determine a security category and applying an assessment of the system's and organization's mission using tools such as mission-impact reports, asset criticality assessment reports, and business impact analyses results in a rating describing the estimated impact to the system and organization should a threat successfully exploit a vulnerability. While impact can be described using either a quantitative or qualitative approach, in the context of IT systems and data, impact is generally described in qualitative terms. As with the ratings used to describe likelihood, impact levels are described using the terms of high, moderate, and low. NIST SP 800-30 provides definitions for the impact ratings of low, medium, and high.

10.1.4.4   Risk Determination

Once the ratings for likelihood and impact have been determined through appropriate analyses, the level of risk to the system and the organization can be derived by multiplying the ratings assigned for threat likelihood (e.g., probability) and threat impact. Table 10-1 shows how to calculate an overall risk rating using inputs from the threat likelihood and impact categories using a 3X3 matrix. Depending on the requirements of the system and the granularity of risk assessment desired, 4x4 and 5x5 matrices may be used instead. The latter can include a Very Low/Very High threat likelihood and a Very Low/Very High threat impact to generate a Very Low/Very High risk level. A Very High risk level may require possible system shutdown or stopping all information system integration and testing effort.

Table 10-1. Risk Level Matrix

Threat Likelihood	Impact		
	Low (10)	Moderate (50)	High (100)
High (1.0)	10 x 1.0 = 10	50 x 1.0 = 50	100 x 1.0 = 100
Moderate (0.5)	10 x 0.5 = 5	50 x 0.5 = 25	100 x 0.5 = 50
Low (0.1)	10 x 0.1 = 1	50 x 0.1 = 5	100 x 0.1 = 10

Risk Scale: High (>50 to 100)   Moderate (>10 to 50)   Low (1 to 10)

01527a

Because the determination of risk ratings for impact and threat likelihood is largely subjective, it is best to assign each rating a numeric value for ease of calculation. The rationale for this justification can be explained in terms of the probability assigned for each threat likelihood level and a value assigned for each impact level. For example:

- The probability assigned for each threat likelihood level is 1.0 for high, 0.5 for moderate, and 0.1 for low.
- The value assigned for each impact level is 100 for high, 50 for moderate, and 10 for low.

Table 10-2, below, describes the risk levels shown in the above matrix. This risk scale, with its ratings of high, moderate, and low, represents the degree of risk to which an information system, facility, or procedure might be exposed if a given vulnerability were exploited. It also describes the type of action senior managers must take for each risk level.

Table 10-2. Risk Scale and Necessary Management Action

Risk Level	Risk Description and Necessary Management Action
High	If an observation or finding is evaluated as high risk, there is a strong need for corrective measures. An existing system may continue to operate, but a corrective action plan must be put in place as soon as possible.
Moderate	If an observation is rated as moderate risk, corrective actions are needed and a plan must be developed to incorporate these actions within a reasonable period of time.
Low	If an observation is described as low risk, the system's authorizing official must determine whether corrective actions are still required or decide to accept the risk.

10.1.5 Step 5 – Control Recommendations

The goal of the control recommendations is to reduce the level of risk to the information system and its data to a level the organization deems acceptable. These recommendations are essential input for the risk mitigation process, during which the recommended procedural and technical security controls are evaluated, prioritized, and implemented. This step is designed to help agencies identify and select controls appropriate to the organization's operations and mission that could mitigate or eliminate the risks identified in the preceding steps. The following factors should be considered in recommending controls and alternative solutions to minimize or eliminate identified risks:

- Effectiveness of recommended options (e.g., system compatibility);
- Legislation and regulation;

- Organizational policy;
- Operational impact; and
- Safety and reliability.

Agencies should consult NIST SP 800-53 for further guidance on the development of control recommendations.

10.1.6 Step 6 – Results Documentation

The risk assessment report is the mechanism used to formally report the results of all risk assessment activities. The intended function of this report is to describe and document the risk posture of the system while it is operating in its stated environment (as described in the system characterization) and to provide organization managers with sufficient information so that they can make sound, risk-based decisions, such as resources that must be allocated to the risk mitigation phase. Lastly, the agency should ensure that the results of the risk assessment are appropriately reflected in the system's Plan of Action and Milestones (POA&M) and System Security Plan.

At a minimum, the risk assessment report should describe the following:

- Scope of the assessment based on the system characterization;
- Methodology used to conduct the risk assessment;
- Individual observations resulting from conducting the risk assessment; and
- Estimation of the overall risk posture of the system.

10.2 Risk Mitigation

The second phase of the risk management process is risk mitigation. Because it is impractical, if not impossible, to eliminate all risk from a system, risk mitigation strives to prioritize, evaluate, and implement the appropriate risk-reducing controls recommended from the risk assessment process based on the guidance provided in NIST SP 800-53.

System and organizational managers may use several options to reduce the risk to a system. These options are risk assumption; risk avoidance; risk limitation; risk planning, research, and acknowledgement; and risk transference.

Figure 10-4 illustrates a straightforward strategy that can be used to determine whether risk mitigation actions are necessary. Working from each risk identified and analyzed in the first process—risk assessment—managers must then decide whether the risk is acceptable or unacceptable and, subsequently, whether to implement additional controls or not to mitigate unacceptable risks. The first decision box in the figure applies to those threats involving intentional attacks. Natural and unintentional human errors are not considered in this decision-making scheme because there are no associated costs to consider, and so the strategy progresses to the next decision box.

Figure 10-4. Risk Mitigation Strategy

Once the decision has been made on which risks are to be addressed in the risk mitigation process, a seven-step approach is used to guide the selection of security controls:

1. Prioritize actions;
2. Evaluate recommended control options;
3. Conduct cost-benefit analyses;
4. Select controls;
5. Assign responsibility;
6. Develop a safeguard implementation plan; and
7. Implement selected control(s).

The process of selecting controls to mitigate identified risks to an acceptable level is based on the security categorization of the system using the methodology provided in FIPS 199. The security categorization is used in two ways: (1) determines which minimum baseline security controls are selected from NIST SP 800-53, and (2) aids in estimating the level of risk posed by a threat/vulnerability pair identified during the risk assessment (see Chapter 5 of this handbook and NIST SP 800-30 for a discussion on identifying threat/vulnerability pairs). FIPS 200, *Minimum Security Requirements for Federal Information and Information Systems,* mandates the use of NIST SP 800-53 for selecting minimum baseline security controls for government systems. System security controls selected are grouped into one of the three categories of management, operational, or technical controls, and are either preventive or detective in nature.

For new systems, once the security controls for the system have been identified and refined and an initial risk assessment conducted, the selected controls must be implemented. For legacy systems, the security controls that are selected are verified. Organizations can leverage controls used among multiple systems by designating them as common controls where implementation, assessment, and monitoring is conducted at an organizational level or by areas of specific expertise (e.g., human resources, physical security, building management). The system owner must understand who is responsible for implementing these controls and identify the risk that this extension of trust will generate. For information on common controls, see NIST SP 800-53, Revision 1.

Because it is impracticable to eliminate all risk, it is important to note that even after the controls have been selected and implemented, some degree of residual risk will remain. The remaining residual risk should be analyzed to ensure that it is at an acceptable level. For federal agencies, after the appropriate controls have been put in place for the identified risks, the authorizing official will sign a statement accepting any residual risk and either authorize the operation of the new information system or request continued processing of the existing information system. If the residual risk has not been reduced to an acceptable level, the risk management cycle must be repeated to identify a way of lowering the residual risk to an acceptable level.

10.3 Evaluation and Assessment

The third and final phase in the risk management process is evaluation and assessment. The art of risk management in today's dynamic and constantly changing information technology (IT) environments must be ongoing and continuously evolving. Systems are upgraded and expanded, components are improved, and architectures are constantly evolving.

The security control evaluation and assessment, which is conducted during the Security Certification Phase of a system's security certification and accreditation, provides input needed to finalize the risk assessment.[68] The results are used to provide the Authorizing Official with the essential information needed to make a credible, risk-based decision on whether to authorize the operation of the information system. Ideally, the risk assessment activities would be conducted at the same time the system is being certified and accredited. The reuse of assessment data will not only save valuable resources, but also provide the most up-to-date risk information for the authorizing official.

Many of the risk management activities are conducted during a snapshot in time—a static representation of a dynamic environment. All the changes that occur to systems during normal, daily operations have the potential to adversely affect the security of the system in some fashion, and it is the goal of the risk management

---

[68] See NIST SP 800-37, *Guide for the Security Certification and Accreditation of Federal Information Systems,* and Chapter 11, Certification and Accreditation, of this guide for additional guidance on the C&A process.

evaluation and assessment process to ensure that the system continues to operate in a safe and secure manner. This goal can be partially reached by implementing a strong configuration management program.[69] In addition, to monitoring the security of an information system on a continuous basis, agencies must track findings from the security control assessment to ensure they are addressed appropriately and do not continue to pose or introduce new risks to the system.

The process of managing risk permeates the Systems Development Life Cycle (SDLC), beginning with the early stages of project inception through the retirement of the system and its data. From inception forward, agencies should consider the possible threats, vulnerabilities, and risks to the system so that they can better prepare it to operate in its intended environment, securely and effectively, and within a select risk threshold, as deemed acceptable by an agency senior official during the security certification and accreditation process.

Websites:
National Institute of Standards and Technology (NIST) National Vulnerability Database
nvd.nist.gov

www.csrc.nist.gov

United States Computer Emergency Response Team (US-CERT)
http://www.us-cert.gov/

References:
Public Law 107-347 [H.R. 2458], *The E-Government Act of 2002, Title III of this Act is the Federal Information Security Management Act of 2002 (FISMA)*, December 17, 2002.

Office of Management and Budget Circular A-130, *Management of Federal Information Resources*, November 2000.

Federal Information Processing Standard 199, Standards for Security Categorization of Federal Information and Information Systems, February 2004.

Federal Information Processing Standard 200, Minimum Security Requirements for Federal Information and Information Systems, March 2006.

National Institute of Standards and Technology Special Publication 800-53A, *Guide for Assessing the Security Controls in Federal Information Systems (draft), April 2006*

National Institute of Standards and Technology Special Publication 800-30, *Risk Management Guide for Information Technology Systems*, July 2002.

National Institute of Standards and Technology Special Publication 800-37, *Guide for the Security Certification and Accreditation of Federal Information Systems*, May 2004.

National Institute of Standards and Technology Special Publication 800-53, Revision 1, *Recommended Security Controls for Federal Information System,* February 2006.

---

[69] See Chapter 14, Configuration Management, of this guide for additional guidance on configuration management.

National Institute of Standards and Technology Special Publication 800-60, *Guide for Mapping Types of Information and Information Systems to Security Categories*, June 2004.

National Institute of Standards and Technology Special Publication 800-64, *Security Considerations in the Information System Development Life Cycle*, Rev. 1, June 2004.

Chapter 11

11. Certification, Accreditation, and Security Assessments

Security certification and accreditation are important activities that support a risk management process and an integral part of an agency's information security program. The security certification and accreditation process is designed to ensure that an information system will operate with the appropriate management review, that there is ongoing monitoring of security controls, and that reaccreditation occurs periodically.

Required by Office of Management and Budget (OMB) Circular A-130, Appendix III, *Security of Federal Automated Information Resources*, security certification and accreditation serves a function similar to quality control. It is the official management decision given by a senior agency official to authorize operation of an information system and to explicitly accept the risk on behalf of the agency. In this vein, it makes senior officials who accept risk fully accountable for their decisions, and in doing so, encourages diligence in the decision-making process.

The Federal Information Security Management Act (FISMA) and OMB Circular A-130, Appendix III, both require that federal agencies perform IT security risk assessments and prepare security plans for all systems. Both risk assessments and security plans are essential components of the security certification and accreditation process. Whether formal or informal, risk assessments provide much of the data needed to formulate a security plan that addresses the risks identified for a given system. Both the risk assessment and the development and maintenance of a security plan that accurately reflects the security requirements and controls in place for a particular system must be incorporated into the system development life cycle (SDLC).[70]

In addition to risk assessments and system security plans, security assessments have an important role in security accreditation. It is essential that agency officials have the most complete and accurate information possible on the security status of their information systems in order to make timely and sound risk-based decisions. The information and supporting evidence needed for security accreditation are developed during a detailed security evaluation of a system, typically referred to as security certification.

Security certification is a comprehensive assessment of the management, operational, and technical security controls in an information system, made in support of security accreditation, to determine the extent to which the controls are implemented correctly, operating as intended, and producing the desired outcome with respect to meeting the security requirements for the system. The results of a security certification are used to reassess the risks and update the system security plan, thus providing the factual basis for an authorizing official to render a security accreditation decision.

---

[70] See National Institute of Standards and Technology(NIST) Special Publication (SP) 800-64, *Security Considerations in the Information System Development Life Cycle*, and Chapter 3, System Development Life Cycle, of this guide for additional information on the SDLC.

By accrediting an information system, an agency official accepts the risks associated with operating the system and the associated implications on agency operations, agency assets, or agency individuals. Completing a security accreditation ensures that an information system will be operated with appropriate management review, that there is ongoing monitoring of security controls, and that reaccredidation occurs periodically in accordance with federal or agency policy and whenever there is a significant change to the system or its operational environment.

In May, 2004, the Information Technology Laboratory (ITL) published National Institute of Standards and Technology (NIST) Special Publication (SP) 800-37, *Guide for the Security Certification and Accreditation of Federal Information Systems*. It provides specific recommendations on how to certify and accredit information systems, and it is applicable to all federal information systems other than those systems designated as national security systems as defined in 44 United States Code (U.S.C.), Section 3542. 11. State, local, and tribal governments, as well as private sector organizations, are encouraged to use the guidelines, as appropriate. The goals of the guidelines are as follows:

- Enable more consistent, comparable, and repeatable assessments of security controls in federal information systems;

- Promote a better understanding of agency-related mission risks resulting from the operation of information systems; and

- Create more complete, reliable, and trustworthy information for authorizing officials to facilitate more informed security accreditation decisions.

NIST SP 800-37 provides augmented, updated security certification and accreditation information to federal agencies and replaced Federal Information Processing Standard (FIPS) 102, *Guidelines for Computer Security Certification and Accreditation*, September 1983, when it was rescinded in February 2005.

11.1 Certification, Accreditation, and Security Assessments Roles and Responsibilities

While federal agencies have in place widely varied naming conventions/nomenclatures for IT security or security certification and accreditation roles, most basic functions in security certification and accreditation process are essentially the same throughout all agencies.[71] The security certification and accreditation process described in this Special Publication is flexible, allowing each agency to accomplish the intent of the specific tasks within their respective organization.

11.1.1 Chief Information Officer

The chief information officer (CIO) works closely with authorizing officials and their designated representatives to ensure that an agency-wide security program is implemented effectively, including all aspects of the security certification and accreditation program component. The CIO has the following responsibilities in relation to security certification and accreditation:

- Promulgate cost-effective practices such as encouraging maximum reuse and sharing of security-related information to include:

---

[71] See Chapter 2, Governance; Chapter 5, Capital Planning; Chapter 8, Security Planning; and Chapter 14, Configuration Management, of this guide for additional guidance on roles and responsibilities.

- Threat and vulnerability assessments;
- Risk assessments;
- Results from common security control assessments; and
- Any other general information that may be of assistance to information system owners and their supporting security staffs.

- In concert with authorizing official, determine appropriate allocation of resources for security programs and systems; and

- In certain instances, operate as the authorizing official for agency-wide general support systems (GSS) or as co-authorizing official with other senior officials for selected agency systems.

11.1.2 Authorizing Official

The authorizing official (or designated approving/accrediting authority) is a senior management official or executive with the authority to formally assume responsibility for operating an information system at an acceptable level of risk to an agency. It is possible that a particular system may require more than one authorizing official. If so, agreements should be established among the authorizing officials and documented in the system security plan. In most cases, it may be

> **Authorizing Official's Designated Representative**
>
> *The Authorizing Official's Designated Representative can be empowered to act on behalf of the authorizing official in all C&A activities for which the authorizing official is responsible with the following exceptions: 1) rendering the system security accreditation decision, and 2) signing the system security accreditation decision letter.*

advantageous to agree to elect a lead authorizing official to represent the interests of the other authorizing officials. The authorizing official has inherent U.S. government authority and, as such, must be a government employee. The authorizing official has the following responsibilities in relation to security certification and accreditation:

- Oversee the budget and business operations of the system;

- Approve system security requirements, system security plans, and memorandums of understanding (MOU) and/or memorandums of agreement (MOA);

- Make and issue final or interim decision on granting, conditionally granting, or denying authority to operate system; and

- Appoint, if so chosen, a designated representative to act on the authorizing official's behalf in coordinating and carrying out the necessary activities required during the security certification and accreditation of a system.

11.1.3 Senior Agency Information Security Officer

The SAISO (or supporting staff member) may serve as the authorizing official's designated representative. The SAISO serves as the CIO's primary liaison to the agency's authorizing officials, information system owners, and Information System Security Officers (ISSOs).

11.1.4 Information System Owner

The information system owner is responsible for the overall procurement, development, integration, modification, or operation and maintenance of an information system. The information system owner has the following responsibilities in relation to security certification and accreditation:

- Develop and maintain the system security plan;

- Ensure system is deployed and operated according to the agreed-upon security requirements;

- Authorize user access to the information system (and with what types of privileges or access rights);

- Ensure system users and support personnel receive the requisite security training (e.g., instruction in rules of behavior);

- Inform key agency officials of the need to conduct a security certification and accreditation of the information system;

- Ensure appropriate resources are available for the security certification and accreditation effort;

- Provide necessary system-related documentation to the certification agent;

- Take appropriate steps to reduce or eliminate system vulnerabilities identified in the security certification and accreditation process; and

- Assemble the security accreditation package and submit it to authorizing official or authorizing official's designated representative for adjudication.

11.1.5 Information Owner

The information owner has statutory or operational authority for specified information and is responsible for establishing the controls for its generation, collection, processing, dissemination, and disposal. The information owner has the following responsibilities in relation to security certification and accreditation:

- Establish rules for appropriate use and protection of the subject information (e.g., rules of behavior); and

- Communicate level of information assurance required for the system with the appropriate system owner.

11.1.6 Information System Security Officer

The ISSO is responsible to the authorizing official, information system owner, or the SAISO for ensuring that the appropriate operational security posture is maintained for an information system or program. The ISSO has the following responsibilities in relation to security certification and accreditation:

- Serve as the principal advisor to the authorizing official, information system owner, or SAISO on all matters relating to the security of the information system;

- Perform or oversee performance of day-to-day security operations of the system;

- Develop or assist in development of system security policy;

- Ensure compliance with system security policy;

- Coordinate/manage changes to the system with the system owner and the information owner, as necessary;

- Assess security impact of system changes; and

- Develop and update the system security plan.

11.1.7   Certification Agent

The certification agent is either an individual, a group, or an organization responsible for conducting a security certification or a comprehensive assessment of the effectiveness of security controls in an information system. The impartiality and independence of the certification agent are important factors in assessing the credibility of the security assessment results and ensuring that the authorizing official receives the most objective information possible to make an informed, risk-based accreditation decision. The certification agent has the following responsibilities in relation to security certification and accreditation:

- Assess the system security plan to ensure the plan provides applicable security controls prior to initializing the certification process;

- Performs a comprehensive assessment of the management, operational, and technical controls in the information system; and

- Recommend corrective actions to reduce or eliminate vulnerabilities in the information system.

11.1.8   User Representatives

Users are responsible for identifying mission/operational requirements and for complying with the security requirements and security controls described in the system security plan. User representatives are individuals that represent the operational interests of the user community and serve as liaisons for that community throughout the SDLC of the information system. The user representatives assist in the security certification and accreditation process, when needed, to ensure that mission requirements are satisfied while meeting the security requirements and using the security controls defined in the system security plan.

11.2   Delegation of Roles

At the discretion of senior agency officials, certain security certification and accreditation roles may be delegated and, if so, appropriately documented. Agency officials may appoint suitably qualified individuals, including contractors, to perform the activities associated with any security certification and accreditation role with the exception of the CIO and authorizing official. The CIO and authorizing official have inherent U.S. government authority, and those roles should be assigned to government personnel only. Individuals serving in delegated roles are able to operate with the authority of agency officials within the limits defined for the specific security certification and accreditation activities. Agency officials retain ultimate responsibility, however, for the results of actions performed by individuals serving in delegated roles.

11.3 The Security Certification and Accreditation Process

The security certification and accreditation process consists of four distinct phases, each further divided into well-defined tasks and subtasks. The four phases are:

- Initiation Phase;
- Security Certification Phase;
- Security Accreditation Phase; and
- Continuous Monitoring Phase.

The **Initiation phase** consists of three tasks: (1) preparation, (2) notification and resource identification, and (3) system security plan review, analysis, and acceptance. This phase will ensure that the authorizing official and the SAISO agree with the contents of the system security plan before the certification agent begins assessing the security controls in the information system.

The **Security Certification** phase consists of two tasks: (1) security control assessment, and (2) security certification documentation. An information system must meet the minimum security requirements in FIPS 200, *Minimum Security Requirements for Federal Information and Information Systems,* by implementing the appropriate security controls and assurance requirements as described in NIST SP 800-53, *Recommended Security Controls for Federal Information Systems*. System assessments are conducted by examining, reviewing, and testing the implementation of the appropriate security control baseline contained in NIST SP 800-53. The procedures for assessing and reporting the assessment results are contained in NIST SP 800-53A, *Guide for Assessing the Security Controls in Federal Information Systems*.[72]

The security certification phase determines the extent to which the security controls in the information system are implemented correctly, operating as intended, and producing the desired system security posture. This phase also identifies specific actions taken or planned to correct security control deficiencies and to reduce or eliminate known system vulnerabilities. At the conclusion of this phase, the authorizing official should have sufficient data to assess the level of risk the system poses to the agency, and render a security accreditation decision.

The **Security Accreditation** phase consists of two tasks: (1) security accreditation decision and (2) security accreditation documentation. This phase is intended to help the accreditation authority determine whether the remaining known vulnerabilities in the system (after implementing an agreed-upon set of security controls) pose an acceptable level of risk to the agency. After successfully completing this phase, the information system owner will be facing one of three scenarios:

- Formal authorization to operate the information system is granted;
- An interim authorization to operate the information system under specific terms and conditions is granted; or
- Authorization to operate the information system is denied.

The **Continuous Monitoring** phase is discussed in section 11.6.

> **Accreditation Package**
>
> *Typically, the information system owner is responsible for compiling C&A documentation. However, the system owner should work closely with the information owner, the ISSO, and the certification authority to ensure that the package meets all agency requirements.*

11.4 Security Certification Documentation

The security certification and accreditation process, in its entirety, culminates in a risk management decision by an agency official. The security accreditation package documents the results of the security certification and provides the authorizing official with the essential information needed to make a credible, risk-based decision on whether to authorize operation of the information system. The security accreditation package contains the following documents:

- Approved system security plan,
- Security assessment report, and
- Plan of Action and Milestones.

> **Security Plan Contents**
>
> *Documents typically attached or referenced in a security plan include: risk assessment, privacy impact assessment, contingency plan, incident response plan, CM plan, security configuration checklists, and any system interconnection agreement.*

---

[72] The second draft of NIST SP 800-53A was published in April 2006.

The **system security plan** provides an overview of the security requirements for the information system and explains the measures the information system owner has taken or plans to take to comply with those requirements.[73] While not strictly required and left to the discretion of the agency, the plan may contain supporting appendices or as references, other system security documents. Such documents may include the risk assessment, privacy impact assessment, contingency plan, configuration management plan, security configuration checklists, and any system interconnection agreements.

The **security assessment report (SAR)** summarizes the results of the activities undertaken by the certification agent. The security assessment report can also contain a list of recommended corrective actions and the completed system reporting form.

The **POA&M** describes the measures that have been implemented or planned to correct any deficiencies noted during the assessment of the security controls and to reduce or eliminate known system vulnerabilities. Figure 11-1 provides an overview of the key sections of the security accreditation package.

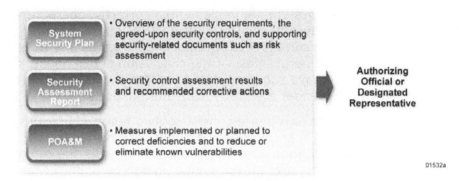

Figure 11-1. Key Security Accreditation Components

11.5 Accreditation Decisions

The security accreditation package documents the results of the security certification. To ensure that the agency's business and operational needs are fully considered, the authorizing official should meet with the system owner prior to issuing the security accreditation decision. In this meeting, the certification and accreditation authorities should clearly explain the rationale for their risk-based decision and, where appropriate, fully explain the terms and conditions of the authorization.

The security accreditation decision communicates the accreditation authority's decision and provides the information system owner with the:

- Security accreditation decision – official decision by the authorizing official on whether to accredit the system, accredit the system with conditions, or deny system accreditation;

---

[73] See NIST 800-18, *Guide for Developing Security Plans for Federal Information Systems,* Revision 1, and Chapter 8, Security Planning, of this guide for additional guidance on system security planning.

- Supporting rationale for the decision – justification for the authorizing official's decision; and
- Terms and conditions for the authorization – limitations or restrictions placed on the operation of the system to which the system owner is bound.

The contents of security certification and accreditation-related documentation, especially information dealing with information system vulnerabilities, should be marked and protected appropriately in accordance with agency policy, and retained in accordance with the agency's record retention policy.

11.6 Continuous Monitoring

The **Continuous Monitoring phase** is an essential component in any security program. During this phase, the status of the security controls in the information system are checked on an ongoing basis. An effective continuous monitoring program can be used to support the annual FISMA requirement for assessing the security controls in information systems. At a minimum, an effective monitoring program requires the following:

- Configuration management and configuration control processes for the information system;
- Security impact analyses on changes to the information system; and
- Assessment of selected security controls in the information system and reporting of information system security status to appropriate agency officials.

To determine which security controls to select for review, agencies should first prioritize testing on POA&M items that become closed. These newly implemented controls should be validated. Agencies should test against system-related security control changes that occurred but did not constitute a major change necessitating a new C&A. Agencies should identify all security controls that are continuously monitored as annual testing and evaluation activities.   Examples of this include (but are not limited to) ongoing security training, Denial of Service and Malicious Code protection activities, Intrusion Detection monitoring, Log File reviews, etc. Once this is completed, agencies should look at the remaining controls that have not been tested for that year and make a decision on further annual testing based on risk, importance of control, and date of last test.

The results of continuous monitoring should be reported to the authorizing official and senior agency information security officer on a regular basis and any necessary updates made to the system security plan. A continuous monitoring reporting form is provided in NIST SP 800-53A.

11.7 Program Assessments

FISMA requires each agency to develop, document, and implement an agency-wide information security program to provide information security for the information and information systems that support the operations and assets of the agency, including those provided or managed by another agency, contractor, or other source.

To ensure the adequacy and effectiveness of information security controls, FISMA requires agency program officials and CIOs to conduct annual reviews of the agency's information security program and report the results to OMB. OMB uses this data to assist in its oversight responsibilities and to prepare an annual report to Congress on agency compliance with FISMA.

In addition, FISMA requires each agency to conduct an independent evaluation of its information security program each year. For agencies with an inspector general (IG), that evaluation is to be done by the agency IG. For agencies without an IG, the evaluation is to be done by an external auditor. In either case, the agency annual report to OMB must include the independent evaluation.

Each quarter, agencies prepare and submit plan of action and milestone (POA&M) reports to OMB for all programs and systems where an information system security weakness has been found. In addition, program officials shall regularly (at the direction of the CIO) update the agency CIO on their program to enable the CIO to monitor agency-wide remediation efforts and provide the quarterly update of the POA&M to OMB.

To assist agencies in meeting their annual FISMA reporting requirements, the Information Security Program Assessment Questionnaire contained in Annex 11.A Agency Information Security Program Assessment Questionnaire, provides questions on many of the areas typically required for inclusion in agency reports. The questionnaire contains agency-wide, program-level questions that are not found in NIST SP 800-53. The questionnaire can be customized with agency-specific, program-related questions and can be completed by the CIO, the senior agency information security officer (SAISO), or an independent assessor who is evaluating the agency information security program.

The questionnaire consists of a cover sheet and a series of questions which are answered for the Agency Information Security Program. The cover sheet requires descriptive information such as the name of the agency, bureau, or agency-operating unit, and the name, title, and organization of the individual completing the questionnaire. The date and time period covered in the report should be listed along with describing the purpose of the assessment. For example, the annual assessment of the agency information security program is required by FISMA; an assessment was performed because of repeated virus infections. The final information listed on the cover sheet is the number of agency systems in the low, moderate, and high FIPS 199 impact categories.

The series of questions are related to the management of an agency-wide information security program. Each of these questions addresses information security program elements critical to the success of an agency information security program. This section is flexible and extensible. The agency may add as many questions as desired to more fully assess the status and/or effectiveness of the agency information security program or to address questions or concerns that are raised by other interested parties.

Each question should be answered for each level of IT Security maturity. For the "Policy" maturity level, to answer "Yes," the topic should be documented in agency policy. For the "Procedures" maturity level, to answer "Yes," the topic should be documented in detailed procedures. For the "Implemented" maturity level, to answer "Yes," the implementation is verified by examining the procedures and program area documentation, and interviewing key personnel to determine that the procedures are implemented. For the "Tested" maturity level, to answer "Yes," documents should be examined and interviews should be conducted to verify that the policies and procedures for the question are implemented and operating as intended and provide the desired level of security. For the "Integrated" maturity level, to answer "Yes," the policies, procedures, implementation, and testing are continually monitored and improvements are made as a normal business process of the agency.

Website:

www.csrc.nist.gov

References:

Public Law 107-347 [H.R. 2458], *The E-Government Act of 2002, Title III of this Act is the Federal Information Security Management Act of 2002 (FISMA)*, December 17, 2002.

Office of Management and Budget Circular A-130, *Management of Federal Information Resources*, November 2000.

Federal Information Processing Standard 199, *Standards for Security Categorization of Federal Information and Information Systems*, February 2004.

Federal Information Processing Standard 200, *Minimum Security Requirements for Federal Information and Information Systems*, March 2006.

National Institute of Standards and Technology Special Publication 800-18, Revision 1, *Guide for Developing Security Plans for Federal Information Systems,* February 2006.

National Institute of Standards and Technology Special Publication 800-53A, *Guide for Assessing the Security Controls in Federal Information Systems (draft), April 2006.*

National Institute of Standards and Technology Special Publication 800-30, *Risk Management Guide for Information Technology Systems*, July 2002.

National Institute of Standards and Technology Special Publication 800-37, *Guide for the Security Certification and Accreditation of Federal Information Systems*, May 2004.

National Institute of Standards and Technology Special Publication 800-53, Revision 1, *Recommended Security Controls for Federal Information System,* February 2006.

National Institute of Standards and Technology Special Publication 800-60, *Guide for Mapping Types of Information and Information Systems to Security Categories*, June 2004.

National Institute of Standards and Technology Special Publication 800-64, *Security Considerations in the Information System Development Life Cycle*, Rev. 1, June 2004.

Annex 11.A Agency Information Security Program Assessment Questionnaire

Name of Agency: _____

Name of Responsible Individual: _____

Name(s) of Assessors: _____

Date of Report: _____

Time Period Covered in Report: _____

Purpose of Report: _____

Agency System Summary:

Number of Systems in each FIPS 199 Impact Level Category

Low: _____ Moderate: _____ High: _____

Information Security Program Questions

Each question should be answered for each level of IT Security maturity. Each column represents an IT Security Maturity Level. For the "Policy" maturity level, to answer "Yes," the topic should be documented in agency policy. For the "Procedures" maturity level, to answer "Yes," the topic should be documented in detailed procedures. For the "Implemented" maturity level, to answer "Yes," the implementation is verified by examining the procedures and program area documentation, and interviewing key personnel to determine that the procedures are implemented. For the "Tested" maturity level, to answer "Yes," documents should be examined and interviews should be conducted to verify that the policies and procedures for the question are implemented and operating as intended and provide the desired level of security. For the "Integrated" maturity level, to answer "Yes," the policies, procedures, implementation, and testing are continually monitored and improvements are made as a normal business process of the agency.

Program Questions	Policy	Procedures	Implemented	Tested	Integrated	Comments
1. Security Control Review Process Does management ensure that corrective information security actions are tracked using the Plan of Action & Milestones (POA&M) process?						
2. Capital Planning and Investment Control Does the agency require the use of a business case/Exhibit 300/Exhibit 53 to record the resources required for security at an acceptable level of risk for all programs and systems in the agency?						
3. Investment Review Board Is there an Investment Review Board (or similar group) designated and empowered to ensure that all investment requests include the security resources needed or that all exceptions to this requirement are documented?						
4. Integrating Information Security and Critical Infrastructure Protection into Capital Planning and Investment Control Is there integration of information security and Critical Infrastructure Protection (CIP) into the Capital Planning and Investment Control(CPIC) Process?						

Program Questions	Policy	Procedures	Implemented	Tested	Integrated	Comments
5. Budget and Resources Are information security resources (internal FTEs and funding) allocated to protect information and information systems in accordance with assessed risks?						
6. Systems and Projects Inventory Are IT projects and systems identified in an inventory and is the information about the IT projects and systems relevant to the investment management process? Is there an inventory of systems as required by FISMA?						
7. IT Security Metrics Are IT security metrics collected agency-wide and reported?						
8. Enterprise Architecture and the Federal Enterprise Architecture Security and Privacy Profile Are system- and enterprise-level information security and privacy requirements and capabilities documented within the agency's Enterprise Architecture? Is that information used to understand the current risks to the agency's mission? Is that information used to help program and agency executives select the best security and privacy solutions to enable the mission?[74]						
9. Critical Infrastructure Protection Plan If required in your agency, is there a documented critical infrastructure and key resources protection plan that meets the requirements of HSPD-7						
10. Life Cycle Management Is there a system life cycle management process that requires each system to be C&A? Is each system officially approved to operate? Is the						

---

[74] http://cio.gov/documents/Security_and_Privacy_Profile_v2.pdf

Program Questions	Policy	Procedures	Implemented	Tested	Integrated	Comments
system LCM process communicated to appropriate persons?						

FISMA requires each agency to appoint a Senior Agency Information Security Officer (SAISO) who heads an office with the mission and resources to develop and maintain an agency information security program. A "Yes" response affirms compliance. A "No" response should be accompanied by explanatory comments and a date when this will be done.

Question	Accomplished?	Comments
Senior Agency Information Security Officer Has a senior agency information security officer been appointed with the mission and resources to develop and maintain an agency information security program?		

Annex 11.B Minimum Security Controls

Security controls in the security control catalog (NIST SP 800-53, Appendix F) have a well-defined organization and structure. The security controls are organized into classes and families for ease of use in the control selection and specification process. There are three general classes of security controls (i.e., management, operational, and technical[75]). Each family contains security controls related to the security function of the family. A standardized, two-character identifier is assigned to uniquely identify each control family. Table 11-1 summarizes the classes and families in the security control catalog and the associated family identifiers.

CLASS	FAMILY	IDENTIFIER
Management	Risk Assessment	RA
Management	Planning	PL
Management	System and Services Acquisition	SA
Management	Certification, Accreditation, and Security Assessments	CA
Operational	Personnel Security	PS
Operational	Physical and Environmental Protection	PE
Operational	Contingency Planning	CP
Operational	Configuration Management	CM
Operational	Maintenance	MA
Operational	System and Information Integrity	SI
Operational	Media Protection	MP
Operational	Incident Response	IR
Operational	Awareness and Training	AT
Technical	Identification and Authentication	IA
Technical	Access Control	AC
Technical	Audit and Accountability	AU
Technical	System and Communications Protection	SC

Table 11-1: Security Control Class, Family, and Identifier

Security control class designations (i.e., management, operational, and technical) are defined below for clarification in preparation of system security plans.

Management controls focus on the management of the information system and the management of risk for a system. They are techniques and concerns that are normally addressed by management. ***Operational controls*** address security methods focusing on mechanisms primarily implemented and executed by people (as opposed to systems). These controls are put in place to improve the security of a particular system (or group of systems). They often require technical or specialized expertise and often rely upon management activities as well as technical controls.

---

[75] Security control families in NIST SP 800-53 are associated with one of three security control classes (i.e., management, operational, technical). Families are assigned to their respective classes based on the dominant characteristics of the controls in that family. Many security controls, however, can be logically associated with more than one class. For example, CP-1, the policy and procedures control from the Contingency Planning family, is listed as an operational control but also has characteristics that are consistent with security management as well.

Technical controls focus on security controls that the computer system executes. The controls can provide automated protection for unauthorized access or misuse, facilitate detection of security violations, and support security requirements for applications and data.

Chapter 12

12. Security Services and Products Acquisition

Information security services and products are essential elements of an organization's information security program. Many products and services to support an agency's information security program for information systems are widely available in the marketplace today, and are frequently used by federal agencies. Security products and services should be selected and used within the organization's overall program to manage the design, development, and maintenance of its information security infrastructure, and to protect its mission-critical information. In the acquisition of both, agencies should apply risk management principles to aide in the identification and mitigation of risks associated with the acquisition.

In the acquisition of information security products, agencies are encouraged to conduct a cost-benefit analysis as part of the product-selection process – one that also includes the costs associated with risk mitigation. This cost-benefit analysis should include a life cycle cost (LCC) estimate for the status quo and one for each identified alternative while highlighting the benefits associated with each alternative. National Institute of Standards and Technology (NIST) Special Publication (SP) 800-36, *Guide to Selecting Information Technology (IT) Security Products*, first defines broad security product categories and specifies product types, product characteristics, and environment considerations within those categories. The guide then provides a list of pertinent questions that agencies should ask when selecting products.

As with the acquisition of products, the acquisition of services bears considerable risks that federal agencies must identify and mitigate. The importance of systematically managing the process for acquisition of information security services cannot be underestimated because of the potential impact associated with those risks. In selecting this type of services, agencies should employ risk management processes in the context of information security services life cycle, which provides an organizational framework for information security decision makers. NIST SP 800-35, *Guide to Information Technology Security Services,* provides assistance with the selection, implementation, and management of information security services by guiding the reader through the various phases of the information security services life cycle. Information security decision makers must consider the costs involved, the underlying security requirements, and the impact of their decisions on the organizational mission, operations, strategic functions, personnel, and service-provider arrangements.

The process of selecting information security products and services involves numerous people throughout an organization. Each person involved in the process, whether on an individual or group level, should understand the importance of security in the organization's information infrastructure and the security impacts of their decisions. Depending on its needs, an organization may include all of the personnel listed below or a combination of particular positions relevant to information security needs.

- Chief Information Officer;
- Contracting Officer;
- Contracting Officer's Technical Representative;
- Information Technology (IT) Investment Review Board (IRB) or its equivalent;
- Security Program Manager;
- Information System Security Officer;
- Program Manager (Owner of Data)/Acquisition Initiator; and
- Privacy Officer.

12.1   Information Security Services Life Cycle

The security services life cycle provides a framework to help security decision makers organize and coordinate their security efforts—from initiation to completion. Figure 12-1 depicts the security services life cycle for obtaining security services at a high level. Table 12-1 provides a brief summary of each phase.

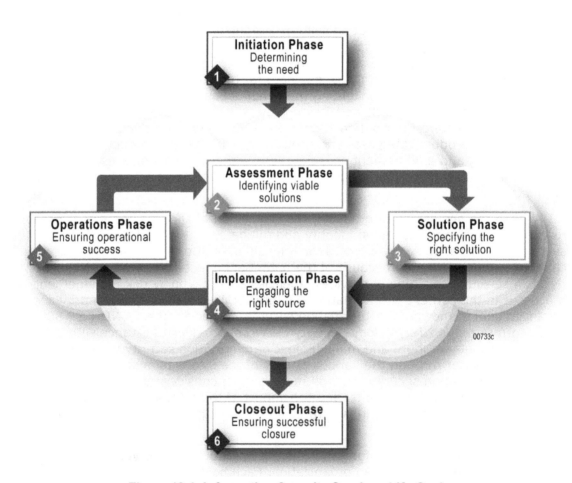

Figure 12-1. Information Security Services Life Cycle

Table 12-1. Information Security Services Life Cycle

Phase	Activity
Phase 1 – Initiation	▪ When the need to initiate the services life cycle is recognized ▪ Consists of needs determination, security categorization, and the preliminary risk assessment
Phase 2 – Assessment	▪ Involves developing an accurate portrait of the current environment before decision makers can implement a service and install a service provider ▪ Baselines the existing environment; metrics creation, gathering, and analysis; total cost of ownership ▪ Analyzes opportunities and barriers ▪ Identifies options and risks
Phase 3 – Solution	▪ Decision makers choose the appropriate solution from the viable options identified during the assessment phase ▪ Develops the business case ▪ Develops the service arrangement ▪ Develops the implementation plan
Phase 4 – Implementation	▪ The service providers are implemented during this phase ▪ Identify the service provider and develop the service agreement ▪ Finalize and execute the implementation plan ▪ Manage expectations
Phase 5 – Operations	▪ The service's life cycle becomes iterative; the service is operational, the service provided is fully installed, and a constant assessment of the service level and source performance must be made ▪ Monitor and measure organization performance ▪ Evaluate and evolve
Phase 6 – Closeout	▪ While unlikely, because of the iterative nature of the life cycle, the service and service provider could continue indefinitely ▪ It is more likely that the environment will change such that information security program managers will identify triggers that will initiate a new and replacement information security service ▪ Select the appropriate exit strategy ▪ Implement the selected exit strategy

12.2 Selecting Information Security Services

Before selecting specific services, organizations should review the current status of their security programs and the security controls that are either planned or in place to protect information systems and data. Organizations should use the risk management process to identify an effective mix of management, operational, and technical security controls that will mitigate risk to an acceptable level. The number and type of appropriate security controls and their corresponding information security services may vary throughout a particular system's services life cycle. The relative maturity of an organization's security architecture is likely to influence the types of security controls that are appropriate for a particular system. The blend of security controls is tied to the mission of the organization and the role of the system within the organization as it supports that mission. A more in-depth look at the various types of security controls can be found in NIST SP 800-53, Revision 1, *Recommended Security Controls for Federal Information Systems,* February 2006. Table 12-2 lists categories of information security services.

Table 12-2. Information Security Services Categories

Categories	Description
Management Services	Techniques and concerns normally addressed by management in the organization's computer security program. They focus on managing the computer security program and the risk within the organization.
Operational Services	Services focused on controls implemented and executed by people (as opposed to systems). They often require technical or specialized expertise and rely on management activities and technical controls.
Technical Services	Technical services focused on security controls a computer system executes. These services are dependent on the proper function of the system for effectiveness.

Selecting the most appropriate services, service mix, and service level is a complex decision, as is deciding who should provide the needed services. A broad range of possible service arrangements exists. An organization may select its internal employees and teams to provide the service required, or it may choose to fully export the service to an external service provider. This external service provider could be any organization, including an external group from a subsidiary organization, a business unit, or a commercial service provider.

12.2.1 Selecting Information Security Services Management Tools

Because of the potential harm caused by inadequate security, information security program managers and decision makers must employ effective management tools to increase the likelihood of success of acquired security services. Two important tools are metrics and service agreements, both of which can be used to make security service providers accountable for the results derived from the services they provide to the organization.

- Metrics are a management tool that facilitates decision making and accountability through practical, relevant data collection, data analysis, and performance data reporting.

- A service agreement is an agreement between the service provider and the organization requesting the service that specifies all services the service provider is to provide, to what extent, the duration of services, etc.

12.2.2 Information Security Services Issues

Implementing a security service and service arrangement can be complex. Each security service carries its own costs and associated risks, as does each service arrangement. Making a decision based on one single issue can have major implications for the organization in other areas. For example, if it becomes clear that an external organization can provide the service more cost-effectively than the current internal service provider, security decision makers will have to consider the implications to the organization's current personnel. The decision makers will have to balance near-term cost/value with potential long-term risks associated with potential loss of employee morale, attrition, and intellectual capital. Table 12-3 provides a list of general factors and issues associated with acquiring security services, grouped into six categories. This list is not intended to be exhaustive; it provides the most common, but not all, related factors and issues.

Table 12-3. Information Security Service Issue Categories

Categories	Issues
Strategic/Mission	For all the importance of security in general and information security in particular, it must support the mission or business function. When thinking about the implications of any decision, ultimately, decision makers must ask themselves what is best for the organization from a strategic point of view and what best helps the organization meet its mission.
Budgetary/Funding	Though funding is often at the heart of any business decision, cost is only one of many issues. The focus should be on value and full life cycle costs.
Technical/ Architectural	IT services, including management services with technical implications. Throughout the life cycle, information security program managers must consider whether their decisions have a technical and architectural effect on the organization.
Organizational	Issues such as damage to an organization's image and reputation, change in focus on core competencies, and resiliency of the organization, relate to the intangible elements of an organization. In many cases, long-accepted internal controls and business practices that have developed over time due to natural business unit divisions or regulatory requirements may have to be reconsidered when an information security service provider is engaged.
Personnel	Issues related to the organization's contractors and employees. Managers must remain aware of the impact of their decisions on their employees. Depending on the service arrangement implemented, major ramifications could exist for current employees; understanding these potential implications and dealing with them early will ensure the employees remain an important resource for the organization.
Policy/Process	Effective security starts with strong policy, and implications to policies and process must be considered to ensure appropriate transitions and implementations.

12.2.3 General Considerations for Information Security Services

In identifying the service provider that best meets an organization's needs, decision makers will need to have many questions answered. Specifically, depending on the nature of the data the service provider accesses and processes on behalf of the agency, the service provider may be subject to legislative and regulatory requirements, including Federal Information Security Management Act (FISMA) and NIST standards and guidance, such as SP 800-53, *Recommended Security Controls for Federal Information Systems*, SP 800-37, *Guide for the Security Certification and Accreditation of Federal Information Systems*, and others. Questions pertaining to these requirements should become part of the organization's standard process for researching and evaluating information security services and service providers. Table 12-4 is a representative sample of such questions, which includes general questions grouped into the six issue categories.

These questions are intended as a guide, and each organization will need to decide which questions are relevant to its specific needs. The questions are not an exhaustive list, and organizations should develop additional questions. Lastly, the question may best be answered by the organization, not the service provider.

Table 12-4. Information Security Service General Considerations

Category	Considerations
Strategic/ Mission	1. What is <*the service provider*>[76] mission? 2. Does <*the service provider*> understand the organization's mission? 3. How does <*the service provider's*> mission and service offering align with and enhance the organization's ability to meet our mission? 4. Describe <*the service provider's*> business, specifying number of staff, customers, locations, and business revenues. Is <*the service provider*> planning any major strategic/mission changes or anticipating any budget/financial viability issues during the period of performance? 5. Is the <*service*> inherently governmental?
Budgetary/ Funding	1. At what cost will <*the service provider*> provide the service? 2. How much would the service cost at a higher service level? At a lower service level? 3. How will <*the service provider*> protect against cost overruns? 4. What remedies would <*the service provider*> offer for cost overruns?
Technical/ Architectural	1. How will <*the service provider*> perform the information security service? 2. Who will provide, i.e., own, the hardware/software needed? 3. At what level will <*the service provider*> provide the service (e.g., percent availability, metrics reports, maintenance, hardware/software refreshment)? 4. How will <*the service provider*> ensure this service level? 5. What remedies would <*the service provider*> consider appropriate (i.e., service credits) for failure to meet the service targets? 6. What are <*the service provider's*> requirements for early termination and extension? 7. How are scale-up/down issues handled? 8. Has <*the service provider*> provided this type of service at this level for this type of organization before? Can <*the service provider*> provide references for those past performance qualifications? 9. What is the information security environment of <*the service provider*>? 10. How would <*the service provider*> handle emergency situations?
Organizational	1. What is <*the service provider's*> work environment and is it compatible with the organization? 2. How well will <*the service provider*> adapt to the organization's environment? 3. What is <*the service provider's*> reputation (in the marketplace and for meeting cost and service targets)? How does <*the service provider*> compare to its competitors?
Personnel	1. Will <*the service provider's*> staff be onsite, offsite, or a mix? 2. Will <*the service provider's*> staff have/be able to obtain the appropriate personnel and facility clearances? 3. What staff will <*the service provider*> assign to this task? What are their skills? 4. How will <*the service provider*> ensure the staff stays current in the technology/service field?
Policy/Process	1. Does <*the service provider*> foresee changes to the organization's policies and/or processes? 2. How do <*the service provider's*> security policies (e.g., contingency planning) differ from that of the organization? If the organization's policy meets a higher standard, will <*the service provider's*> have trouble meeting this higher standard? If lower, will <*the service provider*> abide by the stricter policies of the organization? 3. How does <*the service provider*> address the commingling of its data with that of another organization? Are processes in place to ensure that an organization's data is protected?

---

[76] A word or phrase bounded by '<' and '>' indicates that information should be substituted inside the brackets.

12.3 Selecting Information Security Products

As with security services, before selecting specific products, organizations should review the current status of their security programs and the security controls that are either planned or in place to protect their information and information systems. Table 12-5 lists the general issues for consideration prior to the selection of information security products.

Table 12-5. Information Security Product Selection Considerations

Consideration Type	Considerations
Organizational	▪ Identify the user community ▪ Define the relationship between the security product and the organization's mission ▪ Identify data sensitivity ▪ Identify an organization's security requirements ▪ Review security plan ▪ Review policies and procedures ▪ Identify operational issues such as daily operation, maintenance, and training
Product	▪ Determine total LCC (including acquisition and support) ▪ Assess ease of use ▪ Assess scalability ▪ Identify interoperability requirements ▪ Identify test requirements ▪ Review known vulnerabilities ▪ Test and implement relevant patches ▪ Review product specifications against existing and planned organizational programs, policies, procedures, and standards ▪ Identify security critical dependencies with other products ▪ Investigate the new product's interactions with the existing infrastructure
Vendor	▪ Determine whether the selection of a particular product will limit future security choices ▪ Assess vendor experience and viability ▪ Explore vendor history in responding to security flaws in its products

To facilitate identification and review of these considerations, security program managers may use a set of questions when considering security products for their programs. Table 12-6 lists questions that are product-independent and should be posed during the product selection phase. These questions are organized into three categories: those that apply to the organization, those that apply to the product or its operation, and those that apply to the vendor. It should be noted, however, that these questions are neither exhaustive nor relevant in all circumstances. Organizations should use these questions as a guide, and edit and supplement the questions as required by their unique circumstances in addition to ensuring that their decisions are consistent with their architecture and a well-established business case.

Table 12-6. Information Security Product Selection Questions

Consideration Type	Questions	Comments
Organizational	▪ Is the anticipated user community identified?	
Organizational	▪ How many and what type of users does the organization anticipate will use the security product?	
Organizational	▪ Is the relationship between this security product and the organization's mission performance understood and documented?	

119

Consideration Type	Questions	Comments
Organizational	▪ Has the sensitivity of the data the organization is trying to protect been determined?	In the case of cryptographic modules, where agencies have determined the need to protect information via cryptographic means, they may only select products compliant with cryptographic module validation program (CMVP).
Organizational	▪ Are the organization security requirements supported by the security plan, policies, and procedures?	
Organizational	▪ Have security requirements been identified and compared against product specifications?	
Organizational	▪ Has appropriate contract language been used for the specific product under selection?	
Organizational	▪ Have operational issues such as daily operation, maintenance, contingency planning, awareness and training, and documentation been considered?	
Organizational	▪ Have policies been developed for the procurement and use of evaluated products as appropriate?	Organizations should give consideration to acquisition and deployment of information security products that have been evaluated and tested by independent accredited laboratories against appropriate security specifications and requirements. Examples of these specifications include protection profiles based on ISO/IEC 15408, the *Common Criteria for IT Security Evaluation.*[77] However, agencies should consider their overall requirements and select products accordingly.
Organizational	▪ Is communication required across a domain boundary (implies the need for a boundary controller; e.g., subsystem of firewall, intrusion detection system, and/or routers)?	
Organizational	▪ Are the system components (hardware or software) required for this product identified?	
Organizational	▪ Is the security product consistent with physical security and other policy requirements?	
Organizational	▪ Has the impact on the enterprise operational environment where this product will operate been considered?	
Organizational	▪ Has the impact of emerging technologies on the product been considered?	
Organizational	▪ Is the product necessary to mitigate risk?	When selecting IT products, organizations need to consider the threat environment and the security functions needed to cost effectively mitigate the risks to an acceptable level.
Organizational	▪ Are the system components (hardware or software) required for the identified product?	
Organizational	▪ Have security reviews included requirements for support, plug-in components, or middleware?	
Product	▪ Have total life cycle support, ease-of-use, scalability, and interoperability requirements been determined?	The total life cycle covers "cradle to grave" and hence includes security product disposal requirements.

---

[77] Product considerations for Common Criteria, National Information Assurance Partnership (NIAP) CMVP are further addressed in NIST SP 800-23, *Guidelines to Federal Organizations on Security Assurance and Acquisition/Use of Testing/Evaluated Products.*

Consideration Type	Questions	Comments
Product	• Have test requirements for acceptance and integration testing and configuration management (CM) been developed?	If the product has been evaluated under the National Information Assurance Partnership Common Criteria Evaluation and Validation Scheme (NIAP-CCEVS), validation test reports can be examined to avoid duplication of tests already performed as part of the independent evaluation process.
Product	• Have known product vulnerabilities been addressed by reviewing the relevant vulnerabilities for a product?	Known vulnerabilities for many products can be found using the NIST National Vulnerability Database (NVD) (http://nvd.nist.gov) (formerly known as I-CAT)
Product	• Have all relevant patches been tested and implemented?	
Product	• Have Common Criteria (CC) protection profiles been reviewed, when available (http://www.commoncriteria.org/protection_profiles/pp.html), to identify protection profiles that express security requirements applicable to the organization's needs in the anticipated threat environment?	If existing protection profiles are not adequate, consider the usefulness of similar protection profiles as a starting point for examining products that might satisfy requirements applicable to the new environment.
Product	• Has the CC Centralized Certified Product List been reviewed?	The CC Centralized Certified Product List should be reviewed to ensure that evaluated products are used whenever appropriate. Products independently tested and validated (or mutually recognized) under NIAP-CCEVS with some level of security assurance that the security functions of the product work as specified. In general, third-party testing and evaluation can provide a significantly greater basis for customer confidence that is available from unevaluated products. Note, however, that purchasing an evaluated product simply because it is evaluated and without due consideration of applicable functional and assurance requirements and vendor reliability may be neither useful nor cost effective. Organizations should consider their overall requirements and select the best products accordingly.
Product	• Have the FIPS 140-2 program Validated Products lists been reviewed?	Federal Information Processing Standard (FIPS) 140-2 program Validated Products lists should be reviewed to ensure that evaluated products are used whenever required.
Product	• Has the vendor's policy or stance on revalidating products when new releases of the product are issued been considered?	
Product	• Have product specifications been reviewed with respect to existing and planned organizational programs, policies, procedures, and standards?	Examples include an organization's Web policy, public key infrastructure (PKI) program and policy, Smart Card program, and network interconnection and approval policy.
Product	• Does the product have any security critical dependencies on other products?	For example, an operating system or cryptographic module.
Product	• Does interfacing the new product with the existing infrastructure introduce new vulnerabilities or interdependencies?	

Consideration Type	Questions	Comments
Product	▪ What is the frequency of product failures and adequacy of corrective actions?	
Vendor	▪ Will the selection of a particular product limit the future choices of other computer security or operational modifications and improvements?	Note: the change and pace of technology may make it difficult to estimate the impact to an organization's future security architecture.
Vendor	▪ Does the vendor have experience in producing high quality information security products?	
Vendor	▪ What is the vendor's "track record" in responding to security flaws in its products?	
Vendor	▪ How does the vendor handle software and hardware maintenance, end-user support, and maintenance agreements?	
Vendor	▪ What is the long-term viability of the vendor?	
Vendor	▪ Has the vendor developed a security configuration guide?	
Vendor	▪ Does the vendor have an associated security guide for the product?	
Vendor	▪ Does the vendor use or make reference to NIST, consortia, or other consensus-based checklists, security configurations/settings, or benchmarks?	

Some examples of product types include access control, intrusion detection and other information security-related products. Before deciding to purchase any type of security product, decision makers should consider product capabilities, compatibility with other products, and environmental considerations, among others.

12.4 Security Checklists for IT Products

Vulnerabilities in IT products surface nearly every day, and many ready-to-use exploits are widely available on the Internet. Because IT products are often intended for a wide variety of audiences, restrictive security controls are usually not enabled by default, so many IT products are immediately vulnerable out of the box. Security program managers should review the NIST SP 800-70, *Security Configuration Checklists Program for IT Products,* May 2005, which helps to facilitate the development and dissemination of security checklists so that organizations and individual users can better secure their IT products. A security configuration checklist (sometimes called a lockdown or hardening guide or benchmark) is, in its simplest form, a series of instructions for configuring a product to a particular operating environment.

12.5 Organizational Conflict of Interest

An organizational conflict of interest (OCI) may exist when a party to an agreement has a past, present, or future interest related to the work performed (or to be performed), which may diminish its capacity to provide technically sound, objective service or which may result in an unfair competitive advantage. Agencies should do their best to avoid organizational conflicts before they arise. However, if an organization determines that an OCI exists but cannot be avoided and the organization wishes to proceed nonetheless, the head of the organization must formally waive the OCI.

Identifying the existence of OCIs, mitigating the effect of the OCI to an acceptable level, or waiving the OCI are important steps for consideration when managing the information security service life cycle. However, each of these is a complex matter involving legal and regulatory issues and, as such, should not be considered without the counsel of an organization's legal department.

Website:
http://www.csrc.nist.gov/

References:
National Institute of Standards and Technology Special Publication 800-35, *Guide to Information Technology Security Services*, October 2003.

National Institute of Standards and Technology Special Publication 800-36, *Guide to Selecting Information Technology Security Products*, October 2003.

National Institute of Standards and Technology Special Publication 800-53, Revision 1, *Recommended Security Controls for Federal Information Systems*, February 2006.

National Institute of Standards and Technology Special Publication 800-55, *Security Metrics Guide for Information Technology Systems*, July 2003.

National Institute of Standards and Technology Special Publication 800-64, *Security Considerations in the Information System Development Life Cycle*, Rev. 1, June 2004.

National Institute of Standards and Technology Special Publication 800-70, *Security Configuration Checklists Program for IT Products – Guidance for Checklists Users and Developers*, May 2005.

National Institute of Standards and Technology ITL Bulletin: *Selecting Information Technology Security Products,* April 2004

National Institute of Standards and Technology ITL Bulletin: *Information Technology Security Services; How to Select, Implement, and Manage*, June 2004.

Chapter 13

13. Incident Response

Attacks on information systems and networks have become more numerous, sophisticated, and severe in recent years. While preventing such attacks would be the ideal course of action for organizations, not all information system security incidents can be prevented. Every organization that depends on information systems and networks to carry out its mission should identify and assess the risks to its systems and its information and reduce those risks to an acceptable level.[78] An important component of this risk management process is the trending analysis of past computer security incidents and identifying effective ways to deal with them. A well-defined incident response capability helps the organization detect incidents rapidly, minimize loss and destruction, identify weaknesses, and restore information technology (IT) operations rapidly.

The Federal Information Security Management Act (FISMA) specifically directs federal agencies to develop and implement procedures for detecting, reporting, and responding to security incidents. In addition, OMB[79] directs federal agencies to identify in their FISMA report any incidents (physical or electronic) involving the loss of or unauthorized access to personally identifiable information (PII) and report them according to the policies outlined in OMB Memorandum.[80] Federal civilian agencies are responsible for reporting all computer security incidents to the United States Computer Emergency Response Team (US-CERT) in the Department of Homeland Security and for documenting the corrective actions taken and their impact. Specifically, agencies are responsible for reporting all incidents involving PII to the (US-CERT) within one hour of discovering the incident. Further, policy guidance issued by the OMB in Circular No. A-130, Appendix III, requires that agencies have a capability to provide help to users after a system security incident occurs, and to share information concerning common vulnerabilities and threats.

National Institute of Standards and Technology (NIST) Special Publication (SP) 800-61, *Computer Security Incident Handling Guide*, details a four-phase incident

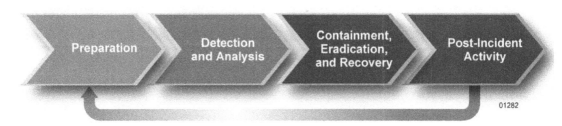

Figure 13-1. Incident Response Life Cycle

---

[78] See NIST Federal Information Processing Standard (FIPS) 199, *Standards for Security Categorization of Federal Information and Information Systems*; NIST 800-30, *Risk Management Guide for Information Technology Systems*; Chapter 10, Risk Management; and Chapter 11, Certification, Accreditation, and Security Assessments, of this guide for additional guidance on system classification and risk management.

[79] OMB, M-06-20, 'FY 2006 Reporting Instructions for the Federal Information Security Management Act and Agency Privacy Management.'

[80] OMB, M-06-19, 'Reporting Incidents Involving Personally Identifiable Information and Incorporating the Cost for Security in Agency Information Technology Investments.'

response process. The major phases of the incident response process—preparation, detection and analysis, containment/eradication/recovery, and post-incident activity, are described in detail throughout the rest of this chapter. Figure 13-1 illustrates the incident response life cycle.

13.1 Preparation

Incident preparation involves not only establishing an incident response capability so that the organization is ready to respond to incidents but also preventing incidents by ensuring that systems, networks, and applications are afforded sufficient security. Incident prevention is now considered a fundamental component of incident response programs, also known as incident management programs, although the incident response team is not typically responsible for it. The incident response team's expertise should be used to establish recommendations for securing systems and preventing incidents, as much as possible. This section provides an overview of actions needed to prevent and handle incidents, including incident data collection preparation.

13.1.1 Preparing for Incident Response

Organizing an effective incident response capability involves the participation of many people within the organization. Making the right planning and implementation decisions is key to establishing a successful incident response program. One of the first planning tasks should be to develop an organization-specific definition of the term "incident" so that the scope of the term is clear. Additional tasks that should be performed during the preparation phase include the following:

- **Create an Incident Response Policy.** The policy should define what events are considered incidents, establish the organizational structure for incident response, define roles and responsibilities, and list the organization's incident reporting requirements.

- **Develop Incident Response and Reporting Procedures.** Based on the incident response policy, standard operating procedures (SOPs) are a delineation of the specific technical processes, techniques, checklists, and forms used by the incident response team. SOPs should be comprehensive and detailed to ensure that the organization's priorities are properly reflected in response operations. In addition, following standardized response procedures is also an effective way to minimize errors, particularly those that might be caused by incident handling pace and stress. Prior to implementation, the organization should test incident response SOPs in order to validate their accuracy and usefulness. Once validated, the SOPs must be widely disseminated throughout the organization. Incidents can occur in countless and unpredictable ways; therefore, it is impractical to develop comprehensive procedures with step-by-step instructions for handling every incident. The best that the organization can do is prepare to handle any type of incident, and more specifically, to handle common types of incidents.

- **Establish Guidelines for Communicating with External Parties.** During the incident response process, the organization may need to communicate with outside parties, including other incident response teams, law enforcement, the media, vendors, and external victims. Because such communications often need to occur quickly, organizations should have predetermined communication guidelines so that only the appropriate information is shared with the right parties. If sensitive information is inappropriately released, it can lead to greater disruption and financial loss than the incident itself. Creating and maintaining a list of internal and external points of contact (POC), along with backups for each contact, should assist in making communications among parties easier and faster.

- **Define Incident Response Team Services.** Although the main focus of an incident response team is performing incident response, most teams offer additional services. Examples of the types of services an incident response team can provide to the organization include security advisory distribution, vulnerability assessment, intrusion detection, and education and awareness.

- **Select a Team Structure and Staffing Model.** The organization should select the team structure and staffing model best suited to its needs. When contemplating the best team structure and staffing model, an organization should considers several factors, such as size of the organization, the geographic diversity of major computing resources, the need for 24/7 availability, cost, and staff expertise.

- **Staff and Train the Incident Response Team.** Members of the incident response team should have excellent technical and problem-solving skills because they are critical to the team's success. Excellent teamwork, organizational, communication, and speaking skills are important as well. Most incident response teams have a team manager and a deputy team manager who assumes authority in the absence of the team manager. In addition, some teams also have a technical lead who assumes oversight of and final responsibility for the quality of the technical work performed by the entire incident response team. Also, larger teams often assign an incident lead as the primary POC for handling a specific incident.

Organizations typically find it challenging to maintain situational awareness for handling large-scale incidents because of their complexity. Many people within the organization may play a role in the incident response, and the organization may need to communicate rapidly and efficiently with various external groups. Collecting, organizing, and analyzing all the pieces of information so that the right decisions can be made and executed are not easy tasks. The key to maintaining situational awareness is to prepare thoroughly to handle large-scale incidents. Two specific actions that support this matter are as follows:

- **Establish and Maintain Accurate Notification Mechanisms.** Organizations should establish, document, maintain, and exercise on-hour and off-hour contact and notification mechanisms for various individuals and groups within the organization (e.g., chief information officer [CIO], head of information security, IT support, business continuity planning) and outside the organization (e.g., incident response organizations, counterparts at other organizations).

- **Develop Written Guidelines for Prioritizing Incidents.** Incident response teams should handle each incident with the appropriate priority, based on the criticality of the affected resources and the current and potential technical effect of the incident. For example, data destruction on a user workstation might result in a minor loss of productivity, whereas root compromise of a public Web server might result in a major loss of revenue, productivity, access to services, and reputation, as well as the release of confidential data (e.g., credit card numbers, social security numbers). Because incident responders normally work under stressful conditions ripe for human error, it is important to clearly define and articulate the incident handling priority process. The incident handling priority process should include a description of how the incident response team should react under various circumstances, as well as a service-level agreement (SLA) that documents appropriate actions and maximum response times. This prioritization should facilitate faster and more consistent decision making.

13.1.2 Preparing to Collect Incident Data

Organizations should be prepared to collect a set of objective and subjective data for each incident. Over time, the incident data collected by the organization can be used for many ends. For example, data on the total number of hours the incident response team has dedicated to incident response activities and its cost over a particular period of time, may be used to justify additional funding of the incident response team. A study of incident characteristics may reveal systemic security weaknesses and threats, changes in incident trends, or other data that can be used in support of the risk assessment process. Another good use of the data is measuring the success of the incident response team. If incident data is collected and stored properly, it should provide several measures of the success (or at least the activities) of the incident response team. Furthermore, organizations that are required to report incident information will need to collect the necessary data to meet their requirements (e.g., FISMA reporting of annual incident statistics).[81]

In the process of preparing to collect incident data, organizations should focus on collecting data that is actionable, rather than collecting data simply because it is available. Absolute numbers are not informative—understanding how they represent threats to and vulnerabilities of the business processes of the organization is what matters. Organizations should decide what incident data to collect based on reporting requirements and on the expected return on investment from the data (e.g., identifying a new threat and mitigating the related vulnerabilities before they can be exploited).

13.1.3 Preventing Incidents

Preventing problems is normally less costly and more effective than reacting to them after they occur. Thus, incident prevention is an important complement to an incident response capability. If security controls are insufficient, high volumes of incidents may occur, overwhelming the resources and capacity for response, which would result in delayed or incomplete recovery, possibly more extensive damage, and longer periods of service unavailability. Incident handling can be performed more effectively if organizations complement their incident response capability with adequate resources to actively maintain the security of networks, systems, and applications. This process is intended to reduce the frequency of incidents, thereby allowing the incident response team to focus on handling serious incidents. Examples of practices that help to prevent incidents are as follows:

- Having a patch management program to assist system administrators in identifying, acquiring, testing, and deploying patches that eliminate known vulnerabilities in systems and applications;
- Hardening all hosts appropriately to eliminate vulnerabilities and configuration weaknesses;
- Configuring the network perimeter to deny all activity that is not expressly permitted;

---

[81] See Chapter 7, Performance Measures, for additional guidance on collecting and reporting incident data.

- Deploying software throughout the organization to detect and stop malicious code; and
- Making users aware of policies and procedures on the appropriate use of networks, systems, and applications.

13.2 Detection and Analysis

Detection and analysis are, for many organizations, the most challenging aspects of the incident response process, in other words, accurately detecting and assessing possible incidents—determining whether an incident has occurred and, if so, the type, extent, and magnitude of the problem. Incidents can be detected through many different means, with varying levels of detail and fidelity. Automated detection capabilities include network-based and host-based intrusion detection systems (IDSs), antivirus software, and log analyzers. Incidents may also be detected through manual means, such as user reports. Some incidents have overt signs that can be easily detected, whereas others are virtually undetectable without automation.

In a typical organization, the thousands or millions of possible signs of incidents that occur any given day are recorded mainly by computer security software. Automation is needed to perform an initial analysis of the data and select events of interest for human review. Event correlation software and centralized logging can be of great value in automating the analysis process. However, the effectiveness of the process depends on the quality of the data that goes into it. Organizations should establish logging standards and procedures to ensure that adequate information is collected by logs and security software and that the data is reviewed regularly. Proper and efficient reviews of incident-related data require people with extensive, specialized technical knowledge and experience.

When a potential incident is identified, the incident response team should work quickly to analyze and validate it, documenting each step taken. The team should rapidly perform an initial analysis to determine the incident's scope, attack methods, and targeted vulnerabilities. This analysis should provide enough information for the team to prioritize subsequent activities, including the containment of the incident. When in doubt, incident handlers should assume the worst until additional analyses indicate otherwise. In addition to prioritization guidelines, organizations should also establish an escalation process for those instances when the incident response team fails to respond to an incident within the designated time.

The incident response team should maintain records about the status of incidents, along with other pertinent information. Using an application or database for this purpose is necessary to ensure that incidents are handled and resolved in a timely manner. The incident response team should safeguard this data and other data related to incidents because it often contains sensitive information concerning recent security breaches, exploited vulnerabilities, and users that may have performed inappropriate actions.

13.3 Containment, Eradication, and Recovery

It is important to contain an incident before it spreads to avoid overwhelming resources and increasing damage caused by the incident. Most incidents require containment, so it is important to consider it early in the course of handling each incident. An essential part of containment is decision making, such as shutting down a system, disconnecting it from the network, or disabling certain system functions. Such decisions are much easier to make if strategies and procedures for containing the incident have been predetermined. Organizations should define acceptable risks in dealing with incidents and develop strategies accordingly.

Containment strategies vary based on the type of incident. For example, the overall strategy for containing an e-mail-borne virus infection is quite different from that of a network-based distributed denial of service attack. Organizations should create separate containment strategies for each major type of incident. The criteria for choosing the appropriate strategy should be documented clearly to facilitate quick and effective decision making. Examples of criteria include potential damage to and theft of resources, the need to preserve evidence, the effectiveness of the strategy, the time and resources needed to implement the strategy, and the duration of the solution.

After an incident has been contained, eradication may be necessary to eliminate components of the incident, such as deleting malicious code and disabling breached user accounts. For some incidents, eradication is either unnecessary or is performed during recovery. In recovery, administrators restore systems to normal operation and (if applicable) harden systems to prevent similar incidents. Recovery may involve such actions as:

- Restoring systems from clean backups;
- Rebuilding systems from scratch;
- Replacing compromised files with clean versions;
- Installing patches;
- Changing passwords; and
- Tightening network perimeter security (e.g., firewall rule sets).

It is also often desirable to employ higher levels of system logging or network monitoring as part of the recovery process. Once a resource is successfully attacked, it is often attacked again, or other resources within the organization are attacked in a similar manner

13.4 Post-Incident Activity

After a major incident has been handled, the organization should hold a lessons-learned meeting to review the effectiveness of the incident handling process and identify necessary improvements to existing security controls and practices. Lessons-learned meetings should also be held periodically for lesser incidents. The information accumulated from all lessons-learned meetings, as well as the data collected while handling each incident, should be used to identify systemic security weaknesses and deficiencies in policies and procedures. Follow-up reports generated for each resolved incident can be important for evidentiary purposes, used as a reference in handling future incidents, and used in training new incident response team members. An incident database, with detailed information on each incident that occurs, can be another valuable source of information for incident handlers.

Websites:

United States Computer Emergency Response Team (US-CERT)
http://www.us-cert.gov/

www.csrc.nist.gov

References:

Federal Information Processing Standard 199, *Standards for Security Categorization of Federal Information and Information Systems*, February 2004.

National Institute of Standards and Technology Special Publication 800-30, *Risk Management Guide for Information Technology Systems*, July 2002.

National Institute of Standards and Technology Special Publication 800-61, *Computer Security Incident Handling Guide*, January 2003.

Chapter 14

14. Configuration Management

The purpose of Configuration Management (CM) is to manage the effects of changes or differences in configurations on an information system or network. CM assists in streamlining change management processes and prevents changes that could detrimentally affect the security posture of a system before they happen. In its entirety, the CM process reduces the risk that any changes made to a system (insertions/installations, deletions/uninstalling, and modifications) result in a compromise to system or data confidentiality, integrity, or availability in that it provides a repeatable mechanism for effecting system modifications in a controlled environment. In accordance with the CM process, system changes must be tested prior to implementation to observe the effects of the change, thereby minimizing the risk of adverse results.

Each organization must take into account the associated costs and expenses, the required planning and scheduling, and the necessary training associated with a thorough and effective CM process. However, since each general CM approach is universal, agencies can structure and implement a repeatable CM process to save organizational resources on future projects. Additionally, CM helps to eliminate the risk of confusion, problems, and unnecessary spending. The additional resources required to correct a problem that could have been prevented through sound CM practices, is likely to far exceed the amount of resources required to develop and implement an effective enterprise CM process.

National Institute of Standards and Technology (NIST) Special Publication (SP) 800-64, *Security Considerations in the Information System Development Life Cycle,* states "Configuration management and control procedures are critical to establishing an initial baseline of hardware, software, and firmware components for the information system and subsequently to controlling and maintaining an accurate inventory of any changes to the system. Changes to the hardware, software, or firmware of a system can have a significant impact on the security of the system...changes should be documented, and their potential impact on security should be assessed regularly." NIST SP 800-53, Revision 1, *Recommended Security Controls for Federal Information Systems*, defines seven CM controls that organizations are required to implement based on an information system's security categorization. The required CM controls are defined in Table 14-1.[82]

Table 14-1. NIST SP 800-53 CM Control Family

Identifier	Title	Control
CM-1	Configuration Management Policy and Procedures	The organization develops, disseminates, and periodically reviews/updates: (1) a formal, documented CM policy that addresses purpose, scope, roles, responsibilities, and compliance; and (2) formal, documented procedures to facilitate the implementation of the CM policy and associated CM controls.
CM-2	Baseline Configuration	The organization develops, documents, and maintains a current baseline configuration of the information system and an inventory of the system's constituent components.

[82] See NIST SP 800-53, Revision 1, *Recommended Security Controls for Federal Information Systems*, for supplemental guidance and control enhancements associated with the implementation of these controls.

Identifier	Title	Control
CM-3	Configuration Change Control	The organization documents and controls changes to the information system. Appropriate organization officials approve information system changes in accordance with organizational policies and procedures.
CM-4	Monitoring Configuration Changes	The organization monitors changes to the information system and conducts security impact analyses to determine the effects of the changes.
CM-5	Access Restrictions for Change	The organization enforces access restrictions associated with changes to the information system.
CM-6	Configuration Settings	The organization configures the security settings of information technology (IT) products to the most restrictive mode consistent with information system operational requirements.
CM-7	Least Functionality	The organization configures the information system to provide only essential capabilities and specifically prohibits and/or restricts the use of the following functions; ports, protocols, and/or services: [*Assignment: organization-defined list of prohibited and/or restricted functions, ports, protocols, and/or services*]. Information systems are capable of providing a wide variety of functions and services. Some of the functions and services, provided by default, may not be necessary to support essential organizational operations (e.g., key missions, functions). The functions and services provided by information systems should be carefully reviewed to determine which functions and services are candidates for elimination (e.g., voice over internet protocol, instant messaging, file transfer protocol, hyper text transfer protocol, file sharing).

14.1 Configuration Management in the System Development Life Cycle

Although CM is not traditionally regarded as a security function, it must be addressed in the system development life cycle (SDLC)[83] because of its serious security implications. CM is just one component of an information system's security posture. It falls under the operational controls of an information system and is interrelated with numerous other security disciplines such as project management, risk management, security certification and accreditation,[84] and security awareness training.[85]

CM should be addressed throughout the entire life cycle of any given project or task. As mentioned earlier, it is nearly impossible to carry out a systems development or management project with success in the absence of a sound and effective CM process. In the SDLC, the planning of the CM process falls in Phases 2 and 3; the primary implementation of the CM process is performed during Phase 4, the Operations/ Maintenance phase. SDLC and its associated key tasks are depicted in Figure 14-1.

---

[83] See NIST SP 800-64, *Security Considerations in the Information System Development Life Cycle*, and Chapter 3, System Development Life Cycle, of this guide for additional information on the SDLC.
[84] See NIST SP 800-37, *Guide for the Security Certification and Accreditation of Federal Information Systems,* and Chapter 11, Certification, Accreditation, and Security Assessments, of this guide for additional guidance on C&A.
[85] See NIST SP 800-16, *Information Technology Security Training Requirements: A Role- and Performance-Based Model*; NIST SP 800-50, *Building an Information Technology Security Awareness and Training Program;* and Chapter 4, Awareness and Training, of this guide for additional guidance on security awareness and training.

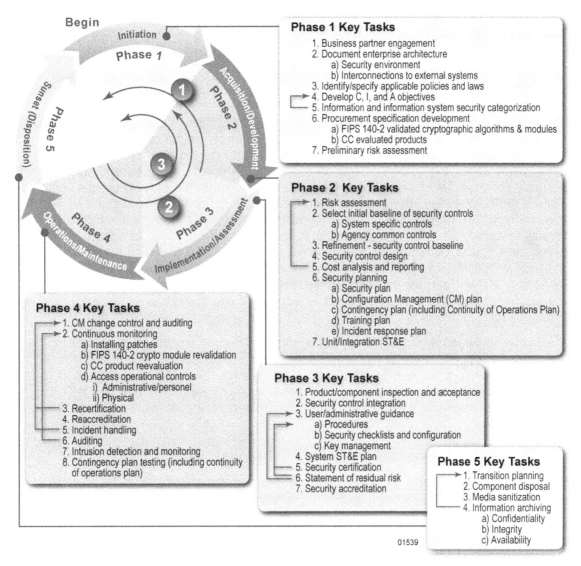

Figure 14-1. System Development Life Cycle

During Phase 2, Acquisition/Development, the risk management process begins with the initial risk assessment. NIST SP 800-30, *Risk Management Guide for Information Technology Systems*, defines risk management as "the process that allows information technology (IT) managers to balance the operational and economic costs of protective measures and achieve gains in mission capability by protecting the information systems and data that support their organizations' missions."[86] Risk management encompasses the process of identifying, analyzing, and responding to risk. This process includes identifying existing vulnerabilities in a system or in its respective components. Since risk is oftentimes an uncertainty on whether or not a given event will occur, an executable plan must be in place if a potential risk is exploited. Risk identification involves determining the possible effect on an information system due to a risk. During this phase, initial baselines of security controls are being selected based on assessing the risk level of a network. After the security controls are established, the CM process can begin. The documented CM

---

[86] See Chapter 10, Risk Management, of this guide for additional guidance on risk management.

process should contain procedures and techniques to change a system without detrimentally impacting it, change any interconnected systems, or change the network while accounting for the established security level of the network.

Through Phase 3, Implementation/Assessment, security controls that are selected in Phase 2 are being tested. Also, the security certification and accreditation process takes place. NIST SP 800-37, *Guide for the Security Certification and Accreditation of Federal Information Systems*, defines security accreditation as "the official management decision given by a senior agency official to authorize operation of an information system and to explicitly accept the risk to agency operations, agency assets, or individuals based on the implementation of an agreed-upon set of security controls." Within the security certification and accreditation process are four phases (Initiation, Security Certification, Security Accreditation, and Continuous Monitoring). The fourth phase, Continuous Monitoring, primarily deals with CM. "With regard to configuration management and control, it is important to document the proposed or actual changes to the information system and to subsequently determine the impact of those proposed or actual changes on the security of the system. .... Documenting information system changes and assessing the potential impact those changes may have on the security of the system is an essential aspect of continuous monitoring and maintaining the security accreditation."[87]

Lastly, in Phase 4, Operations/Maintenance, CM change control and auditing steps take place. If there was a significant change addressed in the CM process, then the system must be recertified and reaccredited. Constant monitoring of the system is performed to identify possible risks to the system so these can be addressed through the risk management, security certification and accreditation, and CM processes.

14.2 Configuration Management Roles and Responsibilities

There are many roles associated with implementing an effective CM process. Note that an individual is not limited to a single role (e.g., an individual can be both the system owner and the CM manager). An organization must ensure that management is aware of proposed changes and verify that a thorough review and approval process is in place. Also, separation of duties must be addressed to ensure that changes are being implemented only after being tested and approved. An example of the roles and responsibilities for a sample CM process are listed below:[88]

- **Chief information officer (CIO)**. The CIO is responsible for setting forth policies concerning CM and implementing CM at the highest level for the organization.

- **System owner**. The system owner serves as the authority for all matters of CM for the system. The system owner is responsible for developing functional requirements and verifying that the requirements are implemented appropriately.

- **Information systems security officer (ISSO)**. The ISSO is primarily responsible for addressing security concerns related to the CM program and for providing expertise and decision support to the Configuration Control Review Board (CCRB).

---

[87] NIST SP 800-37, *Guide for the Security Certification and Accreditation of Federal Information Systems*.

[88] See Chapter 2, Governance, Chapter 5, Capital Planning, Chapter 8, Security Planning, Chapter 11, Certification, Accreditation, and Security Assessments of this guide for additional guidance on roles and responsibilities.

- **CCRB**. CM responsibilities of the CCRB include:

  – Discussing and resolving change requests that require additional funding or resources to implement;
  – Ensuring that change requests do not adversely affect any systems or services related to the system or associated systems, subsystems, and facilities; and
  – Evaluating CM metric information on funding and other CM-related issues.

- **CM manager**. The CM manager is responsible for day-to-day activities, including:

  – Documenting and implementing the CM plan;
  – Establishing system baselines and evaluating controls;
  – Ensuring that proposed changes do not adversely affect agency systems or data;
  – Managing change requests and coordinating implementation of changes;
  – Conducting impact analysis of changes;
  – Approving, denying, or deferring changes;
  – Notifying users of system changes;
  – Ensuring existence of a process for storing, retrieving, and distributing CM materials; and
  – Ensuring that an audit trail of changes is documented and maintained.

- **System users**. System users are responsible for reporting any weaknesses or new requirements that are identified in current versions of the software.

- **Developers**. The developers are responsible for coordinating and working with the CM manager to identify, resolve, and implement controls and other CM issues.

14.3 Configuration Management Process

The CM process identifies the steps required to ensure that all changes are properly requested, evaluated, and authorized. The CM process also provides a detailed, step-by-step procedure for identifying, processing, tracking, and documenting changes. An example CM process is depicted in Figure 14-2.

01540a

Figure 14-2. CM Process

Step 1: Identify Change

The first step of the CM process begins with a person or process associated with the information system identifying a need for a change. The change can be initiated by numerous individuals, such as users or system owners, or they may be identified by audit findings or other reviews. A change may consist of updating the fields or records of a database to upgrading the operating system with the latest security patches. Once the need for a change has been identified, a change request should be submitted to the appropriate decision-making body.

Step 2: Evaluate Change Request

After initiating a change request, the effects that the change may have on the system or other interrelated systems must be evaluated. An impact analysis of the change should be conducted using the following as a guideline:

- Whether the change is viable and improves the performance or the security of the system;
- Whether the change is technically correct, necessary, and feasible within the system constraints;
- Whether system security will be affected by the change;
- Whether associated costs for implementing the change were considered; and
- Whether security components are affected by the change.

Step 3: Implementation Decision

Once the change has been evaluated and tested, one of the following actions should be taken:

- **Approve**. Implementation is authorized and may occur at any time after the appropriate authorization signature has been documented.

- **Deny**. Immediate denial of the request regardless of circumstances and information provided.

- **Defer**. Immediate decision is postponed until further notice. In this situation, additional testing or analysis may be needed before a final decision can be made.

Step 4: Implement Approved Change Request

Once the decision to implement the change has been made, it should be moved from the test environment into production. If required, the personnel updating the production environment should be separate from those individuals that developed the change to provide a greater assurance that unapproved changes do not get implemented into production.

Step 5: Continuous Monitoring

The CM process calls for continuous system monitoring to ensure that it is operating as intended and that implemented changes do not adversely impact either the performance or security posture of the system. Agencies can achieve the goals of continuous system monitoring by performing configuration verification tests to ensure that the selected configuration for a given system has not been altered outside of the established CM process. In addition to configuration verification tests, agencies can also perform system audits. Both configuration verification tests and system audits entail an examination of characteristics of the system and supporting documentation to verify that the configuration meets user needs and ensure that the current configuration is the approved system configuration baseline.

As part of the overall CM process, agencies should also perform patch management activities during this step. Patch management assists in the process of lowering the potential risk to a network by "patching" or repairing known vulnerabilities in any of the network or system environments. Increasingly, vendors are proactive in developing and releasing to the public fixes (or antidotes) to known vulnerabilities, and agencies must remain vigilant to ensure that they capture all relevant fixes as they are released, test their implementation for adverse effects, and implement them if deemed appropriate after testing is concluded. Patching is associated with Phase 4 in the life cycle as well as with Phases 2 and 3. In Phase 2, patch management relates to risk management to prevent any vulnerability from being exploited and compromised. Phase 3 contains the testing to ensure that any change (including the patching) does not negatively impact the system.

Website:
http://www.csrc.nist.gov

References:
National Institute of Standards and Technology Special Publication 800-30, *Risk Management Guide for Information Technology Systems*, July 2002.

National Institute of Standards and Technology Special Publication 800-37, *Guide for the Security Certification and Accreditation of Federal Information Systems,* May 2004.

National Institute of Standards and Technology Special Publication 800-53, *Revision 1, Recommended Security Controls for Federal Information Systems*, February 2006.

National Institute of Standards and Technology Special Publication 800-64, *Security Considerations in the Information System Development Life Cycle*, October 2003.

Appendix A – Acronyms List

BIA	Business Impact Analysis
BLSR	Baseline Security Requirements
BRM	Business Reference Model
BY	Budget Year
C&A	Certification and Accreditation
CC	Common Criteria
CCB	Configuration Control Board
CCEVS	Common Criteria Evaluation and Validation Scheme
CCRB	Configuration Control Review Board
CFO	Chief Financial Officer
CFR	Code of Federal Regulations
CIO	Chief Information Officer
CIP	Critical Infrastructure Protection
CISO	Computer Information Security Officer
CM	Configuration Management
CMVP	Cryptographic Module Validation Program
CNSS	Committee on National Security Systems
COOP	Continuity of Operations
COTS	Commercial off-the-shelf
CPIC	Capital Planning and Investment Control
CSO	Chief Security Officer
CY	Current Year
DAA	Designated Approving Authority
DRM	Data and Information Reference Model
FAM	Financial Audit Manual
FAQ	Frequently Asked Questions
FEA	Federal Enterprise Architecture
FEMA	Federal Emergency Management Agency
FFMIA	Federal Financial Management Improvement Act
FIPS	Federal Information Processing Standard
FISCAM	Federal Information System Controls Audit Manual
FISMA	Federal Information Security Management Act
FITSAF	Federal Information Technology Security Assessment Framework
FMFIA	Federal Managers Financial Integrity Act
GAO	Government Accountability Office
GPEA	Government Paperwork Elimination Act
GPRA	Government Performance and Results Act
GSA	General Services Administration
GSS	General Support System

IA	Information Assurance
IDS	Intrusion Detection System
IEC	International Electrotechnical Commission
IG	Inspector General
IRB	Investment Review Board
IRS	Internal Review Service
ISA	Interconnection Security Agreement
ISD	Instructional System Methodology
ISDN	Integrated Services Digital Network
ISO	International Organization for Standardization
ISSO	Information System Security Officer
IT	Information Technology
ITL	Information Technology Laboratory
KSA	Knowledge, Skills, and Abilities
LAN	Local Area Network
LCC	Life Cycle Cost
MA	Major Application
MAO	Maximum Allowable Outage
MOA	Memorandum of Agreement
MOU	Memorandum of Understanding
NIAP	National Information Assurance Partnership
NIST	National Institute of Standards and Technology
NSA	National Security Agency
NVD	National Vulnerability Database (formerly known as I-CAT)
OCI	Organizational Conflict of Interest
OCIO	Office of the Chief Information Officer
OIG	Office of the Inspector General
OMB	Office of Management and Budget
OPM	Office of Personnel Management
PCIE	President's Council on Integrity and Efficiency
PII	Personally Identifiable Information
P.L.	Public Law
PKI	Public Key Infrastructure
PMA	President's Management Agenda
POA&M	Plan of Action and Milestones
POC	Point of Contact
PRA	Paperwork Reduction Act
PRISMA	Program Review for Information Security Management Assistance
PRM	Performance Reference Model
PY	Prior Year
RTO	Recovery Time Objective
SAISO	Senior Agency Information Security Officer

SANS	SysAdmin, Audit, Network, Security
SDLC	System Development Life Cycle
SLA	Service-Level Agreement
SOP	Standard Operating Procedure
SP	Special Publication
SPP	Security and Privacy Profile
SRM	Service Component Reference Model
ST&E	Security, Test, and Evaluation
TRM	Technical Reference Model
U.S.	United States
U.S.C.	United States Code
UPS	Uninterruptible Power Supply
US-CERT	United States Computer Emergency Readiness Team
VPN	Virtual Private Network
WAN	Wide Area Network

Appendix B – Frequently Asked Questions

B.1 Awareness and Training – Summary of FAQs

Q. Why is a thorough awareness and training program vital to a security program?

Q. What is security awareness?

Q. What is security training?

Q. How can an awareness and training program be established?

Q. How can an organization enhance security awareness?

Q. When should an awareness and training program be changed?

Q. What is role-based training?

Q. How can the support for an awareness and training program be gauged?

Q. How can the effectiveness of an awareness and training program be measured?

Q. What is the difference between various "certificates" that are awarded by vendors, third parties, or universities?

Q. What do "professionalization" and professional development have to do with security?

Q. Why is a thorough awareness and training program vital to a security program?

A. The workforce is the largest component of the information security solution. It comprises the resources that:

- Develop policy and procedures;
- Design and develop applications and systems;
- Implement and monitor security controls;
- Ensure regulatory compliance;
- Manage mission and business objectives; and
- Use the information.

In terms of the total security solution, the importance of the workforce in achieving information security goals and the importance of training as a countermeasure cannot be overstated. Establishing and maintaining a robust and relevant information security awareness and training program, as part of the overall information security program, is the primary conduit for providing the workforce with the information and tools needed to protect an agency's vital information resources. Agencies that continually train their workforce in organizational security policy and role-based security responsibilities will have a higher rate of success in protecting information.

Q. What is security awareness?

A. "Awareness" constitutes the point-of-entry for all employees in pursuing IT security knowledge. Awareness seeks to focus an individual's attention on an issue or a set of issues. Awareness is not training.

Security awareness programs provide a blended solution of activities that promote security, establish accountability, and inform the workforce of security news. Awareness programs continually push the security message to users in a variety of formats and provide security information to users.

Q. What is security training?

A. Security training strives to produce relevant and needed security knowledge and skills within the workforce. Training supports competency development and helps personnel understand and learn how to perform their security role. Security training provides general security courses that are appropriate and applicable to the entire workforce and offers role-based training that is tailored to the specific needs of each security role.

Q. How can an awareness and training program be established?

A. A viable awareness and training program takes time and, if starting from scratch, a phased approach will be best. An awareness and training program can be established by following a five-phase process, designed to populate an awareness and training program:

1. Analysis;
2. Design;
3. Development;
4. Implementation; and
5. Evaluation.

Specific details can be found in NIST SP 800-50, *Building an Information Technology Security Awareness and Training Program,* and NIST SP 800-16, *Information Technology Security Training Requirements: A Role-and Performance-Based Model.*

Q. How can an organization enhance security awareness?

A. An organization can enhance security awareness by establishing a continual program that uses a variety of methods, including:

- **Tools** to promote the security cause, including events, such as a security awareness day promotional materials, and rules of behavior;
- **Communication** of security-related material with users, managers, executives, system owners, and others through activities, such as assessment (as is/to be models), strategic plan, and program implementation;
- **Outreach** to leverage internal and external awareness "best practices," such as Web portals, security e-newsletters, and FAQs; and
- **Metrics** to measure the effectiveness of the awareness program.

Q. When should an awareness and training program be changed?

A. Awareness and training programs should be continually changing to meet the unique needs of your environment, culture, business, and mission. Programs should continue to evolve as new technology and associated security issues emerge. Training needs will shift as new skills and capabilities become necessary to respond to new policy and the resultant architectural and technological changes. A change in the organizational mission and/or objectives will influence ideas on how best to design training solutions and content. Emerging issues, such as homeland defense, will also impact the nature and extent of professional development activities that will be necessary to keep users informed/educated about the latest threats, vulnerabilities, and countermeasures. Finally, as security policies evolve, awareness and training material should reflect these changes.

Q. What is role-based training?

A. Individuals need security training based on their particular job functions. Over time, individuals acquire different roles relative to the use of IT within an organization or as they make a career move to a different organization. Sometimes they will be users of applications, in other instances they may be involved in developing a new system, and in some situations, they may serve on a source selection board to evaluate vendor proposals for IT systems. An individual's security knowledge and skills, and therefore training needs, change as their role changes.

To address this reality, knowledge and skill needs have been categorized by job functions into six role-based specialties, which represent categories of generic organizational roles: Manage, Acquire, Design and Develop, Implement and Operate, and Review and Evaluate. Actual positions within your agency are then assigned to a role to determine the actual training requirements for that position. For example, personnel in positions with duties and tasks for contracting officer, contracting officer's technical representative, and source selection board member would be aligned with the "acquire" role. The authorizing official, information security officer, and inspector general auditor are aligned with the "review and evaluate" role, as they deal primarily with compliance activities.

Q. How can the support for an awareness and training program be gauged?

A. The support for an awareness and training program can be shown through many indicators. A few examples are:

- Key stakeholder demonstrates commitment and support.

- Sufficient funding is budgeted and available to implement the agreed-upon awareness and training strategy.

- Infrastructure to support broad distribution (e.g., Web, e-mail, learning management systems) and posting of security awareness and training materials is funded and implemented.

- Executive/senior-level officials deliver messages to staff about security (e.g., staff meetings, broadcasts to all users by agency head), champion the program, and demonstrate support for training by committing financial resources to the program.

- Executives and managers do not use their status in the organization to avoid security controls that are consistently adhered to by the rank and file.

- Level of attendance at voluntary security forums/briefings/training is consistently high.

Q. How can the effectiveness of an awareness and training program be measured?

A. The effectiveness of an awareness and training program can be shown through many indicators. A few examples are:

- Rampant Internet virus attacks no longer plague an organization.

- Users can identify "spam" e-mail traffic and reduce it.

- FISMA scores improve.

- Scores on pre-awareness assessments indicate retention of security knowledge from prior year.

- Personnel are more responsive/proficient in performing their security duties.

- Personnel at all levels demonstrate a minimum level of security literacy.

- Personnel are less susceptible to social engineering.

- Users are implementing stronger passwords.

Q. What is the difference between "certificates" that are awarded by vendors, third parties, or universities?

A. There are distinct differences among training "certifications" that are offered by a variety of organizations. Primarily, one will encounter certificates of completion, certifications awarded by an industry and/or vendors, and graduate-level certificates awarded by academic institutions:

- **Certificates of completion** are provided to individuals to verify that they attended a course—these certificates do not make any claims that the individual actually gained knowledge and/or skills.

- **Industry and vendor certification** require a solid combination of training, education, and experience. These certifications validate knowledge and skills through testing—they provide varying degrees of assurance that an individual has a baseline level of knowledge, skills, and abilities with regard to a predefined body of knowledge. The preparatory work for knowledge- or skill-based certifications normally includes training in a prescribed body of knowledge or technical curriculum, and is supplemented frequently by on-the-job experience.

- **Graduate certificates** in information assurance (IA) are awarded by an academic institution to individuals who successfully complete all graduation requirements. These graduate certificates generally require 18 to 21 credit hours of academic study, have at least four required courses, allow for one or two electives, and may require a research paper, project, or case study.

Q. What do "professionalization" and professional development have to do with security?

A. Professionalization supports the need for consistency and standardization of policy, processes, and procedures within an agency. For security professionals, this professionalization trend reflects the organizational change that is taking place in all agencies as they place more emphasis on security and realize that security is a full-time job. Professionalization is accomplished through professional development. The movement toward professional development and successful certification is referred to as "professionalization."

Professional development integrates training, education, and experience with some form of assessment that validates knowledge and skills and "certifies" a predefined level of competence. Proper blending of awareness, training, education, experience, and certification promotes professional development, which leads to a high-performance workforce.

B.2   Capital Planning – Summary of FAQs

Q. What is the process for integrating security into the capital planning and investment control process?

Q. What criteria should be evaluated when prioritizing investment planning possibilities?

Q. What is the basis for information security priorities that the organization should consider in all agency investments?

Q. What is the compliance gap?

Q. What is the corrective action impact?

Q What is the Exhibit 300?

Q. What is the Exhibit 53?

Q. What is the relationship between Exhibit 300 and Exhibit 53?

Q. What is the role of the information security program manager regarding integration of information security into the CPIC process?

Q. Is there a process for integrating security into the capital planning and investment control (CPIC) process?

A. Yes. There is a seven-step process for prioritizing security activities and corrective actions:

1. Identify the Baseline;
2. Identify Prioritization Requirements;
3. Conduct Enterprise-Level Prioritization;
4. Conduct System-Level Prioritization;
5. Develop Supporting Materials;
6. Implement Investment Review Board and Portfolio Management; and
7. Submit Exhibit 300s, Exhibit 53, and Conduct Program Management.

Q. What criteria should be evaluated when prioritizing investment planning possibilities?

A. Requirements must be prioritized to address the most pressing security investment needs first. Specific prioritization criteria will vary from agency to agency depending on specific agency mission and goals and applicable legislation and regulations. Priorities may be based on agency mission, Executive Branch guidance such as the President's Management Agenda (PMA), OMB guidance, or other external/internal priorities. Examples of security priorities include certifying and accrediting all systems or implementing public key infrastructure (PKI) throughout the enterprise. It is important to note that OMB/Executive Branch guidance or laws should be ranked highest among these priorities.

Q. What is the basis for information security priorities the organization should consider in all agency investments?

A. Priorities may be based on agency mission, executive branch guidance such as the PMA, OMB guidance, or other external/internal priorities. Examples of security priorities include certifying and accrediting all systems or implementing PKI throughout the enterprise. It is important to note that OMB/executive branch guidance or laws should be ranked highest among these priorities.

Q. What is the compliance gap?

A. The compliance gap is the difference between the desired and actual compliance with the security requirements. For example, if an information system has completed 80 percent of certification and accreditation (C&A) activities, that investment would have a C&A compliance gap of 20 percent. The actual compliance of 80 percent is subtracted from the desired compliance of 100 percent to yield a 20 percent compliance gap. The smaller the compliance gap, the more compliant the system or enterprise control. For key information security activities, this information is part of the FISMA report.

Q. What is the corrective action impact?

A. Corrective action impact is the ratio of compliance gap to corrective action cost. It is calculated by dividing the compliance gap percentage by the cost to implement the corresponding corrective action(s). This ratio provides a proportion of result to cost. The higher the impact proportion, the more "bang for the buck" the corrective action will provide. The resulting proportion is multiplied by 100,000 to facilitate further calculations.

$$\left(\frac{\text{Corrective Action Security Compliance Gap \%}}{\text{Corrective Action Cost}} \right) \times 100,000$$

01529

Q. What is the Exhibit 300?

A. The Exhibit 300 is the capture mechanism for all of the analyses and activities required for full internal (investment review board [IRB], Office of the Chief Information Officer [OCIO]) review. More importantly, the Exhibit 300 is the document that OMB uses to assess investments and ultimately make funding decisions. This document provides OMB with a robust assessment of the investment and is the vehicle for IT investments to justify life cycle and annual funding requests to OMB.

Q. What is the Exhibit 53?

A. The Exhibit 53 provides an overview of the agency's entire IT portfolio by listing every IT investment, life cycle, and budget-year cost information. In addition to containing all investments with Exhibit 300s, the Exhibit 53 contains other IT investments that do not have Exhibit 300s (for example, legacy systems with costs below agency thresholds).

Q. What is the relationship between Exhibit 53 and Exhibit 300?

A. OMB evaluates an agency's Exhibit 53 and Exhibit 300s and determines appropriate funding amounts for the budget year based on the justification articulated. Even though the Exhibit 53 and Exhibit 300s are submitted to OMB each September, the budgeting process is not confined to the late summer months. Planning, acquiring, and executing information security budgets are year-round activities.

Q. What is the role of information security program manager regarding integration of information security into the CPIC process?

A. The security program manager is charged with managing information security throughout the agency. With regard to the CPIC process, the information security program manager:

- Develops and maintains appropriate policies for addressing IT security throughout the investment life cycle;

  o Select Phase

    ▪ Data Sensitivity Analysis
    ▪ Privacy Impact Assessment
    ▪ Risk Assessment
    ▪ System Security Plan
    ▪ Contingency Planning

  o Control Phase

    ▪ Certification and Accreditation (C&A)
    ▪ Plan of Action and Milestones (POA&M)
    ▪ Recertification

  o Evaluate Phase

    ▪ Data Sensitivity and Disposal

- Establishes a process for security personnel to review the Security and Privacy sections of each major investment's Exhibit 300 before submitting to OMB to ensure that the exhibit is accurate and represents the security controls in place in the system; and

- Assists with corrective action prioritization based on agency IT security concerns.

B.3   Interconnecting Systems – Summary of FAQs

Q. *What is an ISA?*
Q. *What are the components of ISA?*
Q. *What is an MOU/MOA?*
Q. *What are the components of MOU/MOA?*
Q. *What is the difference between MOU/MOA and ISA?*
Q. *Is it acceptable to combine the MOU/MOA and the ISA?*
Q. *When does C&A need to occur?*
Q. *How often should security reviews occur?*
Q. *What criteria should the organizations use to establish a baseline of minimum-security controls that must be implemented on each of the interconnecting systems?*
Q. *Do organizations need to update a system security plan?*
Q. *Do individual PC(s) connecting to an application, housed behind a firewall through the Internet, require ISA(s)?*
Q. *Can an ISA be terminated by any of the participating parties?*
Q. *Do both parties need to answer each item in the ISA?*
Q. *Are there any federal requirements regarding ISA?*

Q. **What is an ISA?**

A. An Interconnection Security Agreement (ISA) is an agreement established between the organizations that own and operate connected information systems to document the technical requirements of the interconnection. The ISA is a security document that specifies the requirements for connecting the information systems, describes the security controls that will be used to protect the systems and data, and contains a topographical drawing of the interconnection. It is a commitment between the owners of two systems to abide by specific rules of behavior. These rules are discretionary and should be based on risk.

Q. **What are the components of ISA?**

A. An ISA should contain a cover sheet followed by a document of four numbered sections. The information presented within those four sections should address the need for the interconnection and the security controls required and implemented to protect the confidentiality, integrity, and availability of the systems and data. The extent of the information should be sufficient for the two OAs to make a prudent decision about approving the interconnection. The four sections are as follows:

- Section 1: Interconnection Statement of Requirements;
- Section 2: Systems Security Considerations;
- Section 3: Topological Drawing; and
- Section 4: Signatory Authority.

Q. **What is an MOU/MOA?**

A. A Memorandum of Understanding/Memorandum of Agreement (MOU/MOA) is a document that defines the responsibilities of two or more organizations in establishing, operating, and securing a system interconnection. It defines the purpose of the interconnection, identifies relevant authorities, specifies the responsibilities of each organization, defines the apportionment of costs, and identifies the timeline for terminating or reauthorizing the interconnection. The

MOU/MOA documents the terms and conditions for sharing data and information resources and should be signed by an organizational official.

Q. What are the components of MOU/MOA?

A. Each organization may use its own MOU/MOA format, if appropriate, while keeping in mind that the MOU/MOA is a management document and should not contain technical details of the interconnection. Each section should contain general information. Those details should be addressed separately in the ISA. An MOU/MOA should contain a dated cover sheet with both participating organizations listed. In addition to the cover sheet, the MOU/MOA should contain the following sections:

- Section 1: Supersession
  - If there is a superseded document, the title and date of the document is listed.

- Section 2: Introduction
  - The introduction states the purpose of the memorandum between the parties and what the agreement will govern (e.g., the relationship between "Organization A" and "Organization B").

- Section 3: Authorities
  - An example for this section would be: "The authority for this agreement is based on "Proclamation A" issued by the Agency Head on (date)."

- Section 4: Background
  - In the background, the parties should state the intent of the agreement (e.g., "it is the intent of both parties to this agreement to interconnect the following information systems…").

- Section 5: Communications
  - Frequent formal communications are essential to ensure the successful management and operation of the interconnection. In this section, the parties agree to maintain open lines of communication among designated staff at both the managerial and technical levels.

- Section 6: Purpose of the ISA
  - This section states the purpose of the ISA.

- Section 7: Security Requirement
  - Both parties agree to work together to ensure the joint security of the connected systems and the data they store, process, and transmit, as specified in the ISA. Each party should have identified security controls that apply to the interconnection based on each system's information security categorization and impact level and agree on a mutual set of applicable controls.

- Section 8: Cost Considerations
  - This section describes the terms and conditions of the associated costs of the interconnecting mechanism and/or media.

- Section 9: Timeline
  - This section states the agreement's timeline (e.g., "This agreement will remain in effect for one (1) year after the last date on either signature in the signature block below. After one (1) year, this agreement will expire…").

• Section 10: Signatory Authority

Please note this is an abbreviated description of each section. For more information on each of the sections, please refer to Section 4.12.

Q. What is the difference between ISA and MOU/MOA ?

A. An ISA is used to support an MOU/MOA that establishes the requirements for data exchange between two organizations. The MOU/MOA is used to document the business and legal requirements necessary to support the business relations between the two organizations. The MOU/MOA should not include technical details regarding how the interconnection is established; that is the function of the ISA. An ISA is a distinct security-related document that outlines the technical solution and security requirements for the interconnection. It does not replace an MOU/MOA. As older MOUs/MOAs are updated, they should be changed to refer to the appropriate ISA covering the connectivity addressed by the MOU/MOA. An ISA can be signed only by the two AOs/DAAs (or other authorizing management officials as designated by the organizations involved) whose names appear in Section 4 of the agreement. The ISA should be formally signed before the interconnection is declared operational.

Q. Is it acceptable to combine the MOU/MOA and the ISA?

A. Yes. Organizations may combine ISAs and MOUs/MOAs to simplify their management processes and reduce paperwork. When combining ISAs and MOUs/MOAs, organizations must ensure that the contents and the intent of these two documents remain intact.

Q. When does C&A need to occur?

A. Before interconnecting their information systems, each organization should ensure that its respective system is properly certified and accredited in accordance with federal C&A guidelines. The C&A process is applicable for both emerging systems and those already in production. It involves a series of security-related activities, including developing or updating a system security plan, conducting a risk assessment, preparing a contingency plan, and conducting a security review.

Establishing an interconnection may represent a significant change to the connected systems. Each organization should perform an assessment to determine whether recertification of the new configuration is appropriate.

Q. How often should security reviews occur?

A. One or both organizations should review the security controls for the interconnection at least annually or whenever a significant change occurs to ensure that they are operating properly and are providing appropriate levels of protection.

Q. What criteria should the organizations use to establish a baseline of minimum-security controls that must be implemented on each of the interconnecting systems?

A. The security controls of the interconnected systems should be evaluated and meet the standards of the management, operational, and technical controls of the highest classification between the two in accordance with NIST SP 800-53, *Revision 1, Recommended Security Controls for Federal Information Systems*.

Q. Do organizations need to update a system security plan?

A. Yes. Both organizations should update their system security plans and other relevant documentation at least annually or whenever there is a significant change to their information systems or to the interconnection. Refer to NIST SP 800-18 Revision 1, *Guide for Developing Security Plans for Federal Information Systems*, for information on updating system security plans.

Q. Do individual personal computers (PCs) connecting to an application housed behind a firewall through the Internet require ISA(s)?

A. No. An ISA is an agreement established between **organizations** rather than individual systems. Each system involved in interconnection is governed by an organization's DAA who has the authority to formally assume responsibility for operating a system at an acceptable level of risk.

Q. Can an ISA be terminated by any of the participating parties?

A. Yes. The language in the ISA should stipulate how, when, and by whom the agreement can be terminated. This action item will be decided during the drafting of the agreement.

Q. Do both parties need to answer each item in the ISA?

A. Yes. Both parties need to answer each item even if the item affects only one of the parties.

Q. Are there any federal requirements regarding ISA?

A Yes. ISAs must be addressed by all federal organizations. ISA requirements are set forth by OMB and NIST (in NIST SP 800-53, Revision 1, *Recommended Security Controls for Federal Information Systems*). ISAs are also mentioned in the FY05 FISMA Reporting Guidance. The NIST SP 800-53 requirement states:

"The organization authorizes all connections from the information system to other information systems outside of the accreditation boundary and monitors/controls the system interconnections on an ongoing basis. Appropriate organizational officials approve information system interconnection agreements."

B.4   Performance Measures – Summary of FAQs

Q. How can an organization benefit from metrics?
Q. What are the interdependent components of the security metrics program?
Q. What do information security metrics measure?
Q. What is the difference between developing and implementing a metrics program?
Q. What are the activities that comprise the information security metrics process?
Q. What are the activities that comprise the information security implementation process?
Q. Can the use of a metrics program assist an organization with federal requirements or FISMA?
Q. Metrics help to answer three basic questions, what are they?
Q. How are the different metrics selected?
Q. Can a weighting scale be used during the selection process for metrics?
Q. Are there any specific characteristics that should be defined in each metric?

Q. How can an organization benefit from metrics?

A. Metrics bring multiple benefits to organizations, including:

- Improving accountability for security;

- Enabling management to pinpoint specific technical, operational, or management controls that are not being implemented or are being implemented incorrectly;

- Justifying investment requests using quantitative vs. qualitative data;

- Targeting investments specifically to the areas in need of improvement to maximize investment value; and

- Determining the effectiveness of implemented information security processes, procedures, and controls by relating results of information security activities (e.g., incident data, revenue lost to cyber attacks) to the respective requirements and to information security investments.

Q. What are the interdependent components of the security metrics program?

A. The interdependent components of the security metrics program are:

1. Strong upper-level management support, which establishes a focus on security within the highest levels of the organization;
2. Practical security policies and procedures backed by the authority necessary to enforce compliance. Practical security policies and procedures are defined as those that are attainable and provide meaningful security through appropriate controls. Metrics are not easily obtainable if there are no procedures in place;
3. Quantifiable performance metrics that are designed to capture and provide meaningful performance data. To provide meaningful data, quantifiable security metrics must be based on information security performance goals and objectives, and be easily obtainable and feasible to measure. They must also be repeatable, provide relevant performance trends over time, and be useful for tracking performance and directing resources; and
4. Consistent, periodic analysis of the metrics data to apply lessons learned, improve the effectiveness of existing security controls, and plan future controls to meet new security requirements as they occur. Accurate data

collection must be a priority with stakeholders and users if the collected data is to be meaningful to management and faciliate improvement of the overall security program.

Q. What do information security metrics measure?

A. Metrics measure efficiency and effectiveness, implementation, and impact of security activities.

Q. What is the difference between developing and implementing a metrics program?

A. The metrics development process establishes the initial set of metrics and selects the metrics subset appropriate for an organization at a given time. The metrics program implementation process operates a metrics program that is iterative by nature and ensures that appropriate aspects of information security are measured for a specific time period.

Q. What are the activities that comprise the information security metrics process?

A. The information security metrics development process consists of two major activities:

1. Identification and definition of the current information security program; and
2. Development and selection of specific metrics to measure implementation, efficiency, effectiveness, and the impact of the security controls.

Q. What are the activities that comprise the information security implementation process?

A. The information security implementation process consists of six phases:

1. Prepare for data collection;
2. Collect data and analyze results;
3. Identify corrective actions;
4. Develop business case;
5. Obtain resources; and
6. Apply corrective actions.

Q. Can the use of a metrics program assist an organization with federal requirements or FISMA?

A. Yes. Information security metrics will assist in satisfying the annual FISMA reporting requirement by providing an infrastructure for organized data collection, analysis and reporting. Also, information security metrics can be used as input into Government Accountability Office (GAO) and Inspectors General (IG) audits. Implementation of an information security metrics program will demonstrate agency commitment to proactive security.

Q. Metrics help answer three basic questions, what are they?

A. Metrics are one element of a manager's toolkit for making and substantiating decisions. Metrics are used to answer three basic questions:

1. Am I implementing the tasks for which I am responsible?
2. How efficiently or effectively am I accomplishing those tasks?

3. What impact are those tasks having on the mission of my organization?

Q. How are the different metrics selected?

A. The universe of possible metrics, based on existing policies and procedures, will be quite large. Metrics must be prioritized to ensure that the final set selected for initial implementation has the following qualities:

- Facilitates improvement of high-priority security control implementation. High priority may be defined by the latest GAO or IG reports, results of a risk assessment, or internal organizational goal.

- Uses data that can realistically be obtained from existing processes and data repositories.

- Measures processes that already exist and are relatively stable. Measuring nonexistent or unstable processes will not provide meaningful information about security performance and will, therefore, not be useful for targeting specific aspects of performance.

Metrics can be derived from existing data sources, including C&A, security assessments, POA&M, incident statistics, and agency-initiated or independent reviews.

Q. Can a weighting scale be used during the selection process for metrics?

A. Yes. If weights were assigned to metrics in the *Prepare for Data Collection* phase, these weights should be used to prioritize corrective actions. Alternatively, weights may be assigned to corrective actions in the *Identify Corrective Actions* phase based on the criticality of implementing specific corrective actions, the cost of corrective actions, and the magnitude of corrective actions' impact on the organization's security posture.

Q. Are there any specific characteristics that should be defined in each metric?

A. Once applicable metrics that contain the qualities described above are identified, they will need to be documented with supporting detail, including frequency of data collection, data source, formula for calculation, implementation evidence for measured activity, and guide for metric data interpretation.

B.5 Security Planning – Summary of FAQs

Q. Are specific system security plans for minor applications required?
Q. What are "Rules of Behavior"?
Q. What should be considered when selecting the initial set of security controls?
Q. Can an agency tailor their security control baseline?
Q. After the information system security plan is developed, what is the next step?

Q. Are specific system security plans for minor applications required?

A. No. Specific system security plans for minor applications[89] are not required because the security controls for those applications are typically provided by the general support system (GSS) or major application (MA) in which they operate. In those cases where the minor application is not connected to an MA or GSS, the minor application should be briefly described in a GSS plan that has either a common physical location or is supported by the same organization.

Q. What are "Rules of Behavior"?

A. The rules should state the consequences of inconsistent behavior or noncompliance and identify the formal method used by the organization to document the user's understanding of the rules and associated consequences. The rules of behavior should be made available to all users before they receive authorization for access to the system.

Q. What should be considered when selecting the initial set of security controls?

A. The FIPS 199 impact levels must be considered when the system boundaries are drawn and when selecting the initial set of security controls (i.e., control baseline). The baseline security controls can then be tailored based on an assessment of risk and local conditions including organization-specific security requirements, specific threat information, cost-benefit analyses, the availability of compensating controls, or special circumstances.

Q. Can an agency tailor their security control baseline?

A. Yes. An agency has the flexibility to tailor the security control baseline in accordance with the terms and conditions set forth in the standard. Tailoring activities include (1) the application of scoping guidance, (2) the specification of compensating controls, and (3) the specification of agency-defined parameters in the security controls, where allowed. The system security plan should document all tailoring activities.

Q. After the information system security plan is developed, what is the next step?

A. Once the information system security plan is developed, it is important to periodically assess the plan; review any change in system status, functionality, design, etc.; and ensure that the plan continues to reflect the correct information about the system. This documentation and its accuracy are critical for system certification activity. All plans should be reviewed and updated, if appropriate, at least annually.

---

[89] NIST SP 800-37 defines a minor application as an application, other than a major application, that requires attention to security due to the risk and magnitude of harm resulting from the loss, misuse, or unauthorized access to or modification of the information in the application. Minor applications are typically included as part of a GSS.

B.6 IT Contingency Planning – Summary of FAQs

Q. What is IT contingency planning?
Q. In what time frame must systems and data be recovered and restored when a disruption occurs?
Q. What is the contingency planning policy statement?
Q. What is a business impact analysis (BIA)?
Q. What is maximum allowable outage (MAO)?
Q. What is the recovery time objective (RTO)?
Q. What are the components of the IT contingency plan strategy that must be tested?
Q. Where should backup data be stored?

Q. What is IT contingency planning?

A. IT contingency planning is one modular piece of a larger contingency and continuity-planning program that encompasses IT, business processes, risk management, financial management, crisis communications, safety and security of personnel and property, and continuity of government. Each piece is operative in its own right, but together can create a coordinated synergy that efficiently and effectively protects the entire organization.

Q. In what time frame must systems and data be recovered and restored when a disruption occurs?

A. When a disruption occurs, a recovery strategy must be implemented within the recovery time objective (RTO) period.

Q. What is the contingency planning policy statement?

A. The contingency planning policy statement is the first step in developing an IT contingency plan. This policy may exist at the department, agency, and/or program level of the organization. The statement should define the organizations overall contingency objectives; identify leadership, roles and responsibilities, resource requirements, test, training, and exercise schedules; and plan maintenance schedules and the minimum required backup frequency.

Q. What is a business impact analysis (BIA)?

A. The BIA is a critical step to understanding the information systems components, interdependencies, and potential downtime impacts. The contingency plan strategy and procedures should be designed specifically around the results of the BIA. A BIA is conducted by identifying the system's critical resources. Each critical resource is then further examined to determine how long functionality of the resource could be withheld from the information system before an unacceptable impact is experienced.

Q. What is Maximum Allowable Outage (MAO)?

A. Based on the potential impacts, the amount of time the information system can be without the critical resource then provides a recourse recovery priority around which to plan.

Q. What is the Recovery Time Objective?

A. The balancing point between the MAO and the cost to recover establishes the information system's RTO. Recovery strategies must be created to meet the

RTO. The strategy must also address recovering information system critical components within a priority, as established by their individual RTOs.

Q. What are the components of the IT contingency plan strategy that must be tested?

A. The IT contingency plan strategy testing should include:

1. System recovery on an alternate platform from backup media;
2. Coordination among recovery teams;
3. Internal and external connectivity;
4. System performance using alternate equipment;
5. Restoration of normal operations; and
6. Notification procedures.

Q. Where should backup data be stored?

A. Backed up data should be stored offsite and rotated frequently. Also, stored data should be routinely tested to validate backed-up data integrity.

Q. Should I train and educate my personnel on IT contingency planning?

A. Yes. Personnel selected to execute the IT contingency plan must be trained to perform the procedures. Personnel training should include:

- Purpose of the plan;
- Cross-team coordination and communication;
- Reporting procedures;
- Security requirements;
- Team-specific processes; and
- Individual responsibilities.

Plan exercises should be designed to individually and then collectively examine various components of the entire plan. Exercises may be conducted in a classroom setting: discussing specific components of the plan and/or impact issues; or they may be functional exercises: simulating the recovery using actual replacement equipment, data, and alternate sites.

B.7   Risk Management– Summary of Frequently Asked Questions (FAQs)

Q. What is the principal goal of a risk management process?
Q. How many processes does risk management encompass?
Q. What options do system and organizational managers have to reduce the risk present on the system?
Q. Define risk mitigation and explain what steps are involved to control implementation.
Q. The security controls have been established. Is it possible to proceed to the final step of the risk management process?
Q. What is the formal definition of risk?
Q. Is it possible to calculate the likelihood of a threat exploiting a given vulnerability?
Q. What are the steps in the risk assessment process?
Q. How is a system described?
Q. Are there common threats to a system?
Q. What is a vulnerability?
Q. What are the levels of risk?
Q. How often is the risk assessment process conducted?

Q. What is the principal goal of a risk management process?

A. The principal goal of an organization's risk management process should be to protect the organization and its ability to perform its mission, not just its information assets.

Q. How many processes does risk management encompass?

A. There are three processes of risk management: risk assessment, risk mitigation, and evaluation and assessment. When applied appropriately and with due diligence, the processes should meet the Federal Information Security Management Act (FISMA) requirements of "providing information security protections commensurate with the risk and magnitude of the harm resulting from unauthorized access, use, disclosure, disruption, modification, or destruction of...information...and...information systems" collected by and used by the federal government and "ensuring that information security management processes are integrated with agency strategic and operational planning processes."

Q. What options do system and organizational managers have to reduce the risk present on the system?

A. System and organizational managers may use several options to reduce the risk present on a system. These options are risk assumption, risk avoidance, risk limitation, risk planning, research and acknowledgement, and risk transference.

Q. Define risk mitigation and explain what steps are involved to control implementation.

A. The second process in the overall risk management process is that of risk mitigation. Because it is impractical, if not impossible, to eliminate all risks from a system, risk mitigation strives to prioritize, evaluate, and implement the appropriate risk-reducing controls recommended from the risk assessment process based on NIST SP 800-53 guidance. Once the decision has been made on which risks are to be addressed in the risk mitigation process, a seven-step approach is used to guide control implementation:

1. Prioritize actions;
2. Evaluate recommended control options;
3. Conduct cost-benefit analysis;
4. Select control;
5. Assign responsibility;
6. Develop a safeguard implementation plan; and
7. Implement selected control(s).

Q. The security controls have been established. Is it possible to proceed to the final step of the risk management process?

A. No. It is important to note that even after the controls have been selected and implemented, some degree of residual risk will remain. It is impractical to assume that all risk will be eliminated and the remaining residual risk should be analyzed to ensure that it is at an acceptable level. For federal agencies, after the appropriate controls have been put in place for the identified risks, the authorizing official will sign a statement accepting any residual risk and authorize the operation of the new information system or the continued processing of the existing information system. If the residual risk has not been reduced to an acceptable level, the risk management cycle must be repeated to identify a way of lowering the residual risk to an acceptable level.

Q. What is the formal definition of risk?

A. National Institute of Standards and Technology (NIST) Special Publication (SP) 800-30, *Risk Management Guide for Information Technology Systems*, defines risk as, "a function of the likelihood of a given threat-source's exercising a particular potential vulnerability, and the resulting impact of that adverse event on the organization."

Q. Is it possible to calculate the likelihood of a threat exploiting a given vulnerability?

A. Yes. The likelihood of a given threat successfully exploiting a given vulnerability is estimated by evaluating the threat's motivation, opportunity, and methods for conducting such exploitation. The impact of a successful exploitation is estimated through an analysis of the effect the exploitation can have on the confidentiality, integrity, and availability of the system and the data it processes.

Q. What are the steps in the risk assessment process?

A. The risk assessment process has six steps:

- Step 1: System characterization;
- Step 2: Threat identification;
- Step 3: Vulnerability identification;
- Step 4: Control analysis, likelihood determination, impact analysis, risk determination;
- Step 5: Control recommendations; and
- Step 6: Results documentation.

Q. How is a system described?

A. The system is described in terms of its hardware; software; interfaces to other systems, data, people, mission; and criticality and sensitivity (as previously described using FIPS 199 to determine the system's appropriate security categorization). In addition, the system's functional requirements; security policy and architecture; network topology; information flows; security controls in terms of management, operational, and technical controls; and physical and environmental security mechanisms are described.

Q. Are there common threats to a system?

A. Yes. There are common threat sources that typically apply, regardless of the system that should be evaluated. These common threats can be categorized into three areas: (1) natural threats (e.g., floods, earthquakes, tornadoes, landslides, avalanches, electrical storms), (2) human threats (intentional or unintentional), and (3) environmental threats (e.g., power failure).

Q. What is a vulnerability?

A. NIST SP 800-30 defines vulnerability as "a flaw or weakness in system security procedures, design, implementation, or internal controls that could be exercised (accidentally triggered or intentionally exploited) and result in a security breach or a violation of the system's security policy."

Q. What are the levels of risk?

A. This risk scale, with its ratings of High, Moderate, and Low, represents the degree or level of risk to which an information system, facility, or procedure might be exposed if a given vulnerability were exercised. The risk scale also presents actions that senior management, the mission owners, must take for each risk level. The risk descriptions and associated necessary actions are:

- High: If an observation or finding is evaluated as a high risk, there is a strong need for corrective measures. An existing system may continue to operate, but a corrective action plan must be put in place as soon as possible.

- Moderate: If an observation is rated as moderate risk, corrective actions are needed and a plan must be developed to incorporate these actions within a reasonable period of time.

- Low: If an observation is described as low risk, the system's authorizing official must determine whether corrective actions are still required or decide to accept the risk.

Q. How often is the risk assessment process conducted?

A. As mandated by OMB Circular A-130, the risk assessment process is usually repeated at least every three years for federal agencies. However, risk assessments should be conducted and integrated into the SDLC for information systems, not because it is required by law or regulation, but because it is a good practice and supports the organization's business objectives or mission.

B.8 Certification, Accreditation, and Security Assessments – Summary of Frequently Asked Questions

Q. What is security certification?

Q. What is security accreditation?

Q. Are there any necessary activities to support security accreditation?

Q. What are the phases of the certification and accreditation process?

Q. What is included in a security accreditation package?

Q. What is the Information Security Program Assessment Questionnaire?

Q. Do all the 800-53 security controls need annual testing to satisfy the FISMA annual testing requirement?

Q. What factors should be considered when using an automated system assessment reporting tool?

Q. What key security-related activities should be completed before a system is assessed?

Q. Can the System Reporting Form be customized by the organization?

Q. What is security certification?

A. Security certification is a comprehensive assessment of the management, operational, and technical security controls in an information system, made in support of security accreditation, to determine the extent to which the controls are implemented correctly, operating as intended, and producing the desired outcome with respect to meeting the security requirements for the system. The results of a security certification are used to reassess the risks and update the system security plan, thus providing the factual basis for an authorizing official to render a security accreditation decision.

Q. What is security accreditation?

A. Security accreditation is the official management decision given by a senior agency official to authorize operation of an information system and to explicitly accept the risk to agency operations, agency assets, or individuals based on the implementation of an agreed-upon set of security controls. By accrediting an information system, an agency official accepts responsibility for the security of the system and is fully accountable for any adverse impacts to the agency if a breach of security occurs. Thus, responsibility and accountability are core principles that characterize security accreditation.

Q. Are there any necessary activities to support security accreditation?

A. Yes. The assessment of risk and the development of system security plans are two important activities in an agency's information security program that directly support security accreditation and are required by FISMA and OMB Circular A-130, Appendix III.

Risk assessments influence the development of the security controls for information systems and generate much of the information needed for the associated system security plans. Risk assessments can be accomplished in a variety of ways depending on the specific needs of the agency. The assessment of risk is a process that should be incorporated into the SDLC. At a minimum, documentation should be produced that describes the process used and the results obtained.

System security plans provide an overview of the information security requirements and describe the security controls that are in place or planned for meeting those requirements. System security plans can include as references or attachments, other important security-related documents that are produced as part of an agency's information security program (e.g., risk assessments, contingency plans, incident response plans, security awareness and training plans, information system rules of behavior, configuration management (CM) plans, security configuration checklists, privacy impact assessments, system interconnection agreements).

Q. What are the phases of the C&A process?

A. The security C&A process consists of four distinct phases:

1. Initiation Phase. This phase will ensure that the authorizing official and senior agency information security officer agree with the contents of the system security plan before the certification agent begins assessing the security controls in the information system.
2. Security Certification Phase. This phase will determine the extent to which the security controls in the information system are implemented correctly, operating as intended, and producing the desired outcome with respect to meeting the security requirements for the system.
3. Security Accreditation Phase. This phase will determine whether the remaining known vulnerabilities in the information system (after the implementation of an agreed-upon set of security controls) pose an acceptable level of risk to agency operations, agency assets, or individuals.
4. Continuous Monitoring Phase. This phase will provide regular oversight and monitoring of the security controls in the information system and will inform the authorizing official when changes may impact the security of the system.

Q. What is included in a security accreditation package?

A. The security accreditation package contains the following documents: approved system security plan, the security assessment report, and the POA&M. After these documents are completed, the information system owner submits the final security accreditation package to the authorizing official or a designated representative.

Q. What is the Information Security Program Assessment Questionnaire?

A. To assist agencies in meeting their annual FISMA reporting requirements, the Information Security Program Assessment Questionnaire (Annex 11.A) provides questions on many of the areas typically required for inclusion in agency reports.

Q. Do all the 800-53 security controls need annual testing to satisfy the FISMA annual testing requirement?

A. All 800-53 security controls do not need to be tested to satisfy annual testing and evaluation requirements. Agencies should first prioritize testing on POA&M items that become closed. These newly implemented controls should be validated. Agencies should test against system related security control changes that occurred but did not constitute a major change necessitating a new C&A. Agencies should identify all security controls that are continuously monitored as annual testing and evaluation activities. Examples of this include (but are not limited to) ongoing security training, Denial of Service and Malicious Code protection activities, Intrusion Detection monitoring, Log File reviews, etc. Once this is completed agencies should look at the remaining controls that have not been tested for that year and make a decision on further annual testing based on risk, importance of control and date of last test.

Q. What factors should be considered when using an automated system assessment reporting tool?

A. Automated tools can be used to support the assessment process and provide for easier roll-up of data for internal or external reporting. Factors to consider in using automated tools include:

- Ascertaining the completeness of tool functionality in terms of supporting all components listed in NIST SP 800-53A;

- Determining who will have access to the tools, including specific roles and responsibilities;

- Ensuring that the system processing the tool is secure and is certified and accredited;

- Providing adequate training for those using the tool(s); and

- Establishing technical support capability.

Q. What key security-related activities should be completed before a system is assessed?

A. Before a system is assessed, there are key security-related activities that should be completed. An inventory of all systems should be conducted, and then all systems should be categorized according to their impact on the agency's mission. A determination must then be made as to the boundaries of the system, keeping in mind the impact of the information stored within, processed by, or transmitted by the system(s). A completed GSS or MA security plan, which is required under OMB Circular A-130, Appendix III, should describe the boundaries of the system, the impact level of the data, and the security controls in place or planned for the system.

Q. Can the System Reporting Form be customized by the organization?

A. Yes. The System Reporting Form may be customized by the organization. An organization can add more security controls to those listed for each control family, require more descriptive information, and even pre-mark certain security controls if applicable. Additional columns may be added to reflect the status of the control, e.g., planned action date or location of documentation. The System Reporting Form should not have security controls removed or modified to reduce the effectiveness of the control.

B.9 Security Services and Products Acquisition – Summary of FAQs

Q. *What must be considered when managing a security services project?*
Q. *What are the steps in the security services life cycle?*
Q. *What should take place before selecting a security service?*
Q. *Are there security services categories?*
Q. *What is an organizational conflict of interest (OCI)?*
Q. *What is a service agreement?*
Q: *Why should security products be used?*
Q. *What important steps should be taken while selecting a security product?*
Q. *Who should be involved during the security product selection process?*

Q. What must be considered when managing a security services project?

A. The importance of systematically managing the information security services process cannot be underestimated because of the potential impact on the organization if the many issues involved are not properly considered and the organizational risks are not managed. Information security decision makers must think about not only the costs involved and the underlying security requirements, but also the impact of their decisions on the organizational mission, operations, strategic functions, personnel, and service provider arrangements.

Q. What are the steps in the security services life cycle?

A. The information security services life cycle provides a framework around which the various information security decision makers can organize their information security efforts—from initiation to closeout. The steps for the life cycle are:

1. Initiation Phase: Determining the need;
2. Assessment Phase: Identifying viable solutions;
3. Solution Phase: Specifying the right solution;
4. Implementation Phase: Engaging the right source;
5. Operations Phase: Ensuring operational success; and
6. Closeout Phase: Ensuring successful closure.

Q. What should take place before selecting a security service?

A. Before selecting specific services, organizations should review the current status of their security programs and the security controls that are planned or in place to protect information and information systems. Organizations should use the risk management process to identify the most effective mix of management, operational, and technical security controls that will mitigate risk to an acceptable level. The number and type of appropriate security controls and their corresponding information security services may vary throughout a particular system's services life cycle. The relative maturity of an organization's security architecture may influence the types of appropriate security controls.

Q. Are there security services categories?

A. Yes. Security services are divided into three categories: management, operational, and technical services. Characteristics of each service are listed below:

• Management Services are techniques and concerns normally addressed by management in the organization's computer security program. They focus on managing the computer security program and the risk within the organization.

- Operational Services are focused on controls implemented and executed by people (as opposed to systems). They often require technical or specialized expertise and rely on management activities and technical controls.

- Technical Services are focused on the security controls an information system executes. These services are dependent on the proper function of the system for effectiveness.

Q. What is an organizational conflict of interest (OCI)?

A. An OCI may exist when a party to an agreement has a past, present, or future interest related to the work performed (or to be performed), which may diminish the capacity to provide impartial, technically sound, objective service, or results in an unfair competitive advantage. Of course, it is best to avoid organizational conflicts before they arise.

Q. What is a service agreement?

A. A service agreement is the agreement between the service provider and the organization requesting the service. As service arrangements become more complex and employ commercial service providers, the formality of the agreement should increase. A fully externalized service arrangement with a commercial entity, for example, will require a formal contract so that managers can hold service providers accountable for their actions.

Q. Why should security products be used?

A. Security products should be selected and used within the organization's overall program to manage the design, development, and maintenance of its information security infrastructure, and to protect the confidentiality, integrity, and availability of its mission-critical information.

Q. What important steps should be taken while selecting a security product?

A. It is important to perform a cost-benefit analysis when selecting security products. As part of the cost-benefit analysis, a life cycle cost (LCC) estimate for the status quo and each alternative identified should be developed. In addition to LCC estimates, benefits associated with each alternative should be identified and, to the extent practicable, quantified in terms of dollar savings or cost avoidance. Once the necessary controls are identified, information security products can be identified to provide for these controls.

Q. Who should be involved during the security product selection process?

A. Product selection involves numerous people throughout an organization. Depending on its needs, an organization may include all of the following personnel or a combination of particular positions relevant to information security needs: information security program manager, chief information officer, IT investment review board (or equivalent), program manager/system owner/data, owner/procurement initiator, acquisition personnel, contracting officer, contracting officer's technical representative, or system security officer.

B.10 Incident Response – Summary of FAQs

Q. *What are the four phases of the incident response life cycle?*
Q. *What are some practices that may prevent incidents?*
Q. *What does an incident response capability do?*
Q. *Why is it important to have an incident response capability?*
Q. *What are federal civilian agencies accountable for in terms of reporting security incidents?*
Q. *Is it possible to prepare for incident response?*
Q. *What should be included in the incident response policy?*
Q. *What elements should be considered when selecting a team structure and staffing model?*

Q. What are the four phases of the incident response life cycle?

A. NIST SP 800-61, *Computer Security Incident Handling Guide*, states that the four phases of the incident response life cycle are:

- Preparation;
- Detection and Analysis;
- Containment, Eradication, and Recovery; and
- Post-Incident Recovery.

Q. What are some practices that may prevent incidents?

A. Examples of practices that help to prevent incidents are:

- Having a patch management program to assist system administrators in identifying, acquiring, testing, and deploying patches that eliminate known vulnerabilities in systems and applications;

- Hardening all hosts appropriately to eliminate vulnerabilities and configuration weaknesses;

- Configuring the network perimeter to deny all activity that is not expressly permitted;

- Deploying software throughout the organization to detect and stop malicious code; and

- Making users aware of policies and procedures concerning the appropriate use of networks, systems, and applications.

Q. Why is it important to have an incident response capability?

A. Policy guidance issued by OMB Circular A-130, Appendix III, requires that agencies have a capability to provide help to users when security incidents occur in their systems and to share information concerning common vulnerabilities and threats.

Q. What does an incident response capability do?

A. A well-defined incident response capability helps an organization detect incidents rapidly, minimize losses and destruction, identify weaknesses, and restore IT operations without delay.

Q. What are federal civilian agencies accountable for in terms of reporting security incidents?

A. According to OMB Memorandum 05-15, *FY 2005 Reporting Instructions for the Federal Information Security and Management Act Report and Privacy Management Report* (June 13, 2005), agencies must identify and report the total number of successful incidents in the following categories: unauthorized access, denial of service attacks, malicious code, improper usage, or other, consistent with NIST Special Publication 800-61, *Computer Security Incident Handling Guide* (January 2004). Successful incidents must be recorded and reported internally, to US-CERT, and depending on their severity, to law enforcement. As stated in the US-CERT Concept of Operations, each incident category has a specific timeframe of when it needs to be reported to US-CERT. These time frames are as follows:

- Unauthorized Access: Within one (1) hour of discovery and/or detection;

- Denial of Service: Within two (2) hours of discovery and/or detection;

- Malicious Code: Daily or within one (1) hour if discovery and/or detection is widespread; and

- Improper Usage: On a weekly basis.

In addition, agencies must report Scans/Probes/Attempted Access on a monthly basis or within one (1) hour of discover if it is a classified system.

In addition, a system-specific incident response plan is considered an integral part of a complete system certification and accreditation package.

Q. Is it possible to prepare for incident response?

A. Yes. To prepare for incident response, the organization should do the following:

- Create an organization-specific definition of the term "incident" so that the scope of the term is clear;
- Create an incident response policy;
- Develop incident response and reporting procedures;
- Set guidelines for communicating with external parties;
- Determine incident response team services;
- Select a team structure and staffing model; and
- Staff and train the incident response team.

Q. What should be included in the incident response policy?

A. An incident response policy should define which events are considered incidents, establish the organizational structure for incident response, define roles and responsibilities, and list the requirements for reporting incidents.

Q. What elements should be considered when selecting a team structure and staffing model?

A. The organization should select the appropriate team structure and staffing models based on several factors, including the size of the organization, the geographic diversity of major computing resources, the need for 24/7 availability, cost, and staff expertise.

B.11 Configuration Management (CM) – Summary of FAQs

Q. What is configuration management?
Q. Why is configuration management important?
Q. What should be considered and taken into account when developing a configuration management process?
Q. What steps should be performed before implementing a change?
Q. Is configuration management required by all federal organizations?
Q. Is configuration management a security function?
Q. What are the steps in the configuration management process?
Q. What constitutes a "change"?
Q. What should be evaluated during an impact analysis of the proposed change?
Q. A change has just been implemented, is the job complete?

Q. What is configuration management?

A. NIST SP 800-64, *Security Considerations in the Information System Development Life Cycle,* states, "Configuration management and control procedures are critical to establishing an initial baseline of hardware, software, and firmware components for the information system and subsequently to controlling and maintaining an accurate inventory of any changes to the system. Changes to the hardware, software, or firmware of a system can have a significant impact on the security of the system...changes should be documented, and their potential impact on security should be assessed regularly."

Q. Why is configuration management important?

A. With the complexity and uniqueness of each information system (often due to various user accounts and privileges, department software, or a user's personal preferences), it is difficult for each system to be identically configured to all others on any given network. CM needs to exist to minimize the effects on an information system or network due to these changes or differences in configurations. With multiple system platforms, each differing item (hardware or software) poses a potential vulnerability that can be compromised and significantly affect a network.

Q. What should be taken into account when developing a configuration management process?

A. Each organization must take into account the associated costs and expenses, the required planning and scheduling, and the necessary training associated with a thorough and effective CM process.

Q. What steps should be performed before implementing a change?

A. It is very important to test possible configuration changes before implementing them. The assigned changes should be tested in a controlled environment to ensure minimal risk of an adverse effect.

Q. Is configuration management required by all federal organizations?

A. Yes. CM requirements are set forth by OMB and NIST and must be addressed by all federal organizations. NIST SP 800-53, Revision 1, *Recommended Security Controls for Federal Information Systems*, defines seven CM controls that organizations are required to implement based on an information system's security categorization.

Q. Is configuration management a security function?

A. No. Although not traditionally regarded as a security function, CM needs to be included in the SDLC due to its strong security implications. CM is just one component of an information system's security posture. It falls under the operational controls of an information system and is interrelated with numerous other security disciplines, such as project management, risk management, C&A, and security awareness training.

Q. What are the steps in the configuration management process?

A. The CM process identifies the steps required to ensure all changes are properly requested, evaluated, and authorized. The CM process also provides a detailed, step-by-step procedure for identifying, processing, tracking, and documenting changes. The following steps comprise the CM process:

- Identify change;
- Evaluate change request;
- Implementation decision;
- Implement approved change request; and
- Continuous monitoring.

Q. What constitutes a "change"?

A. A change may consist of various things: from updating the fields or records of a database to upgrading the operating system with the latest security patches.

Q. What should be evaluated during an impact analysis of the proposed change?

A. During an impact analysis, one should look for the following:

- Whether the change is viable and improves the performance or the security of the system;
- Whether the change is technically correct, necessary, and feasible within the system constraints;
- Whether system security will be affected by the change;
- Whether associated costs for implementing the change were given consideration; and
- Whether security components are affected by the change.

Q. A change has just been implemented, is the job complete?

A. No. The system should be continuously monitored to ensure that it is operating as intended and that changes that have been implemented do not have an adverse effect on the performance of the system. Configuration verification and audits should be performed during this step to ensure that the updates to the system have not adversely affected the system. Verification and audits consist of an examination of system characteristics and the supporting documentation to verify that the configuration meets users' needs, and that the current configuration is the approved system configuration baseline.